Ivan Moscovich's
Mastermind Collection

Brain-Flexing
Balance Problems
& Other Puzzles

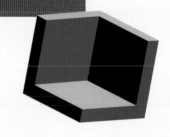

Sterling Publishing Co., Inc.
New York

To Anitta, Hila, and Emilia, with love

Ivan Moscovich's Mastermind Collection:
Brain-Flexing Balance Problems & Other Puzzles was edited, designed, and typeset by
Imagine Puzzles Ltd., London (info@imaginepuzzles.com)

MANAGING EDITOR
David Popey
ART EDITOR
Keith Miller
DESIGNER
Peter Laws
CONSULTANT EDITOR
David Bodycombe
PROJECT EDITOR
Marilyn Inglis
EDITORIAL ASSISTANT
Rosemary Browne
PUBLISHING DIRECTOR
Hal Robinson

Clipart: Nova Development Corporation

Library of Congress Cataloging-in-Publication Data Available

2 4 6 8 10 9 7 5 3 1

Published by Sterling Publishing Co., Inc.
387 Park Avenue South, New York, NY 10016
© 2006 by Ivan Moscovich
Distributed in Canada by Sterling Publishing
c/o Canadian Manda Group, 165 Dufferin Street
Toronto, Ontario, Canada M6K 3H6
Distributed in the United Kingdom by GMC Distribution Services
Castle Place, 166 High Street, Lewes, East Sussex, England BN7 1XU
Distributed in Australia by Capricorn Link (Australia) Pty. Ltd.
P.O. Box 704, Windsor, NSW 2756, Australia

Printed in China

Sterling ISBN-13: 978-1-4027-2733-7
ISBN-10: 1-4027-2733-X

For information about custom editions, special sales, premium and corporate purchases, please
contact Sterling Special Sales Department at 800-805-5489 or specialsales@sterlingpub.com

Contents

Introduction

Ever since my high school days I have loved puzzles and mathematical recreational problems. This love developed into a hobby when, by chance, some time in 1956, I encountered the first issue of *Scientific American* with Martin Gardner's mathematical games column. And for the past 50 years or so I have been designing and inventing teaching aids, puzzles, games, toys, and hands-on science museum exhibits.

Recreational mathematics is mathematics with the emphasis on fun, but, of course, this definition is far too general. The popular fun and pedagogic aspects of recreational mathematics overlap considerably, and there is no clear boundary between recreational and "serious" mathematics. You don't have to be a mathematician to enjoy mathematics. It is just another language, the language of creative thinking and problem-solving, which will enrich your life, like it did and still does mine.

Many people seem convinced that it is possible to get along quite nicely without any mathematical knowledge. This is not so: Mathematics is the basis of all knowledge and the bearer of all high culture. It is never too late to start enjoying and learning the basics of math, which will furnish our all-too sluggish brains with solid mental exercise and provide us with a variety of pleasures to which we may be entirely unaccustomed.

In collecting and creating puzzles, I favor those that are more than just fun, preferring instead puzzles that offer opportunities for intellectual satisfaction and learning experiences, as well as provoking curiosity and creative thinking. To stress these criteria, I call my puzzles Thinkthings.

The *Mastermind Collection* series systematically covers a wide range of mathematical ideas, through a great variety of puzzles, games, problems, and much more, from the best classical puzzles taken from the history of mathematics to many entirely original ideas.

A great effort has been made to make all the puzzles understandable to everybody, though some of the solutions may be hard work. For this reason, the ideas are presented in a highly esthetic visual form, making it easier to perceive the underlying mathematics.

More than ever before, I hope that these books will convey my enthusiasm for and fascination with mathematics and share these with the reader. They combine fun and entertainment with intellectual challenges, through which a great number of ideas, basic concepts common to art, science, and everyday life, can be enjoyed and understood.

Some of the games included are designed so that they can easily be made and played. The structure of many is such that they will excite the mind, suggest new ideas and insights, and pave the way for new modes of thought and creative expression.

Despite the diversity of topics, there is an underlying continuity in the topics included. Each individual Thinkthing can stand alone (even if it is, in fact, related to many others), so you can dip in at will without the frustration of cross-referencing.

I hope you will enjoy the *Mastermind Collection* series and Thinkthings as much as I have enjoyed creating them for you.

—Ivan Moscovich

Five simple mechanisms, which are older than recorded history, provide the basis of all simple machines. The lever, the wheel and axle, the pulley, the wedge, and the screw have made man's working life easier for millennia.

✳ Simple machines—Force and lifting

Machines help us to do work by trading distance for force. Work is using force to move something to push, pull, or lift. The utility of a machine is in its mechanical advantage. The efficiency of a machine is the ratio of its work output and its work input.

The ancient Greeks grouped their contemporary machines into five simple mechanisms or "simple machines" (enumerated by the Greek inventive genius, Hero of Alexandria, around the 1st century BC). They are the lever, the wheel and axle, the pulley, the wedge, and the screw.

The teaching of physics usually starts with the study of mechanics, firstly because mechanical processes lie closest to everyday life's experiences, and secondly because, in the study of mechanics, fundamental principles are learned which are essential for the understanding of processes in many other subjects. Primitive man invented simple devices to overcome gravity, such as wedges and levers, while the ancient Egyptians utilized various combinations of ropes and ramps to move blocks of stone in constructing the pyramids and other massive monuments.

The pulley was probably invented along with the first iron tools. Assyrian reliefs from the 8th century BC show its common uses in Middle Eastern civilizations.

"Give me a place on which to stand and I will move the Earth," said Archimedes, the great Greek mathematician and engineer—and he meant it. Impressed by the enormous magnification of force that can be produced by machines, he claimed to be able to lift the whole planet by a lever if only he could find a suitable balance point as a fulcrum.

Simple machines may be considered as detachable extensions of the human body that supplement the functions of the arms or legs. Variations of these simple machines are everywhere around us today. Originally they merely augmented the muscular efforts of men and animals, but gradually they were incorporated into more and more complex tools and machines that use various types of energy.

A woodcut from *Mechanics Magazine*, London, 1824

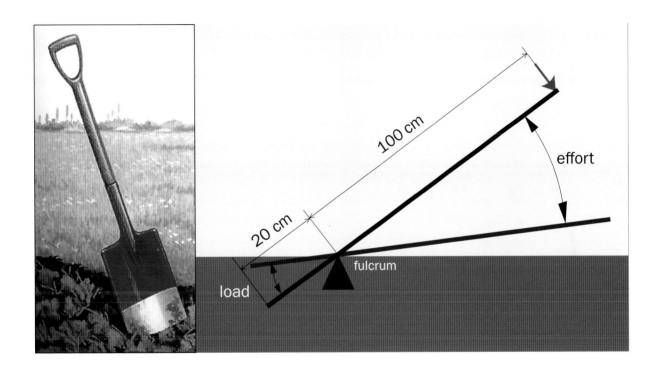

▲ LEVER PRINCIPLE

A lever is probably the simplest example of a "simple machine." It is an energy transformer. Does it give us something for nothing? No. But can you quantify a mathematical relationship between the effort and the load?

ANSWER: PAGE 98

Among his many inventions, Leonardo da Vinci designed what he hoped would be a perpetual motion machine. He inspired many other inventors over time to try to invent a true "perpetuum mobile."

▲ PERPETUAL MOTION MACHINE

Leonardo's design for a "perpetuum mobile." The dream of 100% efficiency in machines spurred on early inventors in the quest for perpetual motion—the creation of a machine which, once started, would continue to run itself and do work until the parts wore out. Can you tell if the above machine would work?

Answer: page 98

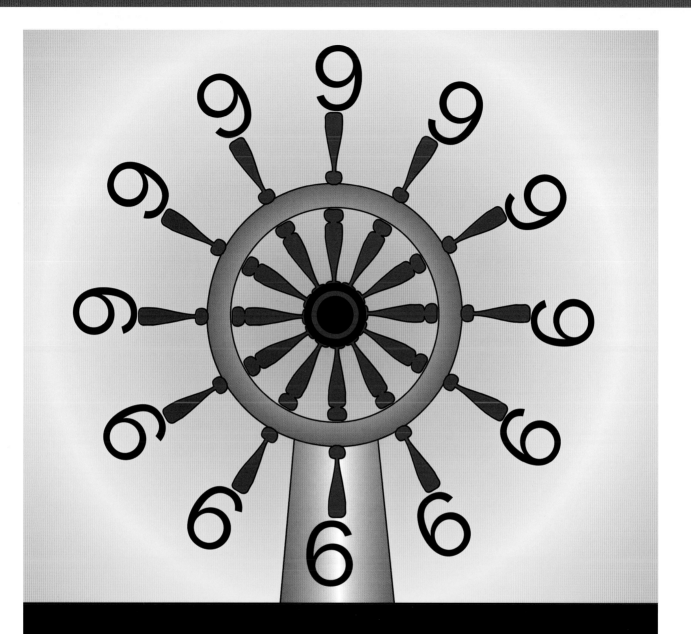

▲ **PERPETUAL MOBILE**

George Gamow, the famous American mathematician, jokingly invented a
perpetual motion machine, depicted above. Can you explain its theoretical
principle of operation? Will it work?

ANSWER: PAGE 98

Basic scientific principles are employed in magic tricks to entertain these days. In ancient times they were employed by priests to produce "real" magic of the gods.

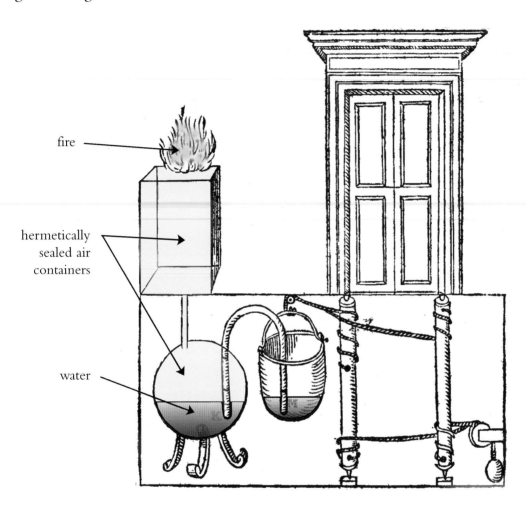

fire

hermetically sealed air containers

water

▲ HERO'S DOOR-OPENING MECHANISM

Some of the most ingenious mechanisms of the ancient world were the inventions of Hero of Alexandria (c. 10–70 AD). He can certainly be considered the first and possibly the greatest toy and gadget inventor from that early age.

The above mechanism for opening a temple door was typical of the many toys and automata he invented that were intended for "magical" purposes. The blueprint, according to Hero's original, shows a mechanism for opening the door of a temple.

Can you tell how it was meant to work?

ANSWER: PAGE 98

▼ MONKEY ON THE ROPE

A classic puzzle by Lewis Carroll:

The monkey and the bananas are in equilibrium.

What will happen to the bananas if the monkey starts climbing the rope?

ANSWER: PAGE 98

▲ LIFT YOURSELF?

Can the girl lift herself by pulling downward on the rope?

ANSWER: PAGE 99

PLATFORM UP

*Can the boy lift himself and the platform
on which he stands by pulling the rope?*

ANSWER: PAGE 99

It is reasonable to suppose that man discovered the roller before the wheel. The difference between the two is important. Unlike the wheel, the roller is independent of the vehicle that it transports.

✳ The revolving circle— how a roller works

As the load on top of the roller is propelled forward, it moves the roller beneath it. The result is that both the load and the roller move forward.

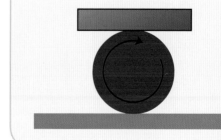

▲ ROLLER PRINCIPLE

Early civilizations around the world independently discovered that rollers could greatly facilitate the transportation of heavy loads. Without this discovery, building pyramids, temples, and giant stone monuments would have been impossible.

The circumference of each of the two rollers is one yard. If the rollers make a full revolution, how much will the weight be carried forward?

ANSWER: PAGE 99

❋ Gears

Rotary motion is the most common type of motion for a machine shaft or axle. One way to transmit rotary motion and force from one axis to another is by using gears.

A gear wheel is a basic mechanism—just a wheel with teeth. Gears are used in practically every machine around us. Their teeth fit into one another so that one gear can turn another but in the opposite direction. Gears are a means of changing the rate of rotation of a machinery shaft. They can change the direction of the axis of rotation, and can also change rotary motion to linear motion. A group of gears is called a gear train.

By using gears of different sizes, the two hands of analog clocks are made to turn at different speeds. A car's gearbox has many gears of different sizes. When you change gear you change the arrangement of the gears to obtain different forward and reverse speeds.

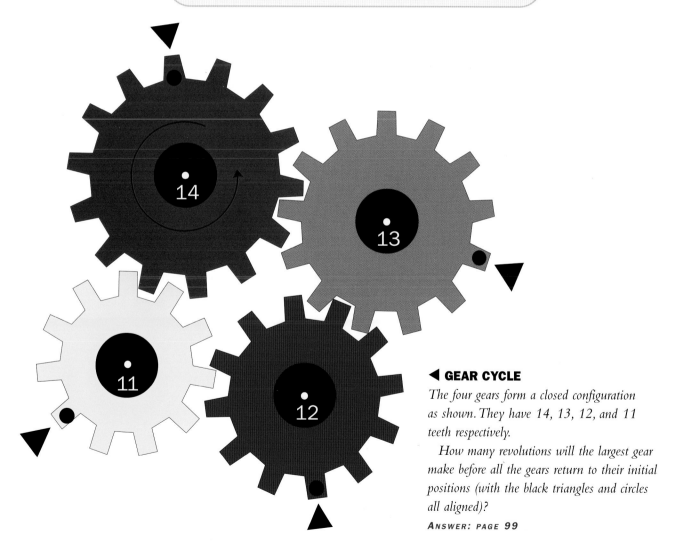

◀ GEAR CYCLE

The four gears form a closed configuration as shown. They have 14, 13, 12, and 11 teeth respectively.

How many revolutions will the largest gear make before all the gears return to their initial positions (with the black triangles and circles all aligned)?

ANSWER: PAGE 99

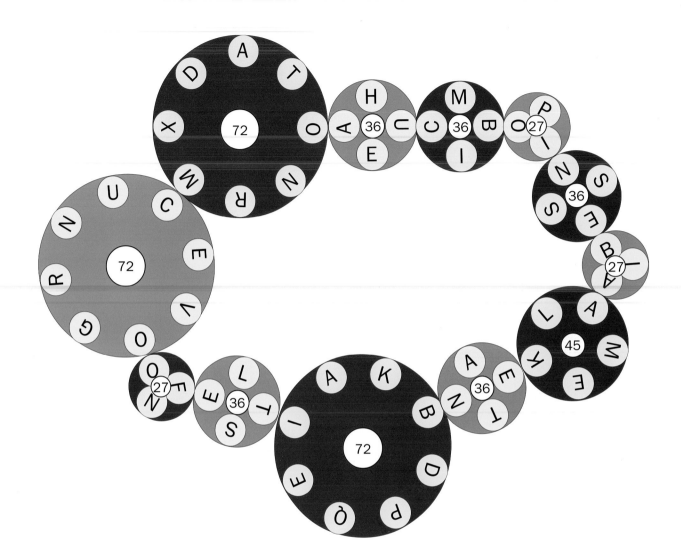

▲ GEAR ANAGRAM

Each of the 12 interlocking gears carry letters around their circumferences. (The number on each gear specifies how many teeth the gear has.) After a certain number of revolutions or partial revolutions, the letters at the contact points of the gears will spell out a sentence starting from the large red gear at the upper left and reading clockwise.

Can you work out how many revolutions the large gear will have to make for you to be able to read the sentence along the contact points of the meshed gears?

ANSWER: PAGE 100

▼ GEAR SWITCHING

The numbers on the gears indicate the number of teeth on each gear.
The small red gear makes 1 full revolution in 12 minutes in a clockwise
direction. The two moving racks will activate two fixed switches as shown.
Can you tell how long it will take for the two switches to be activated?

ANSWER: PAGE **100**

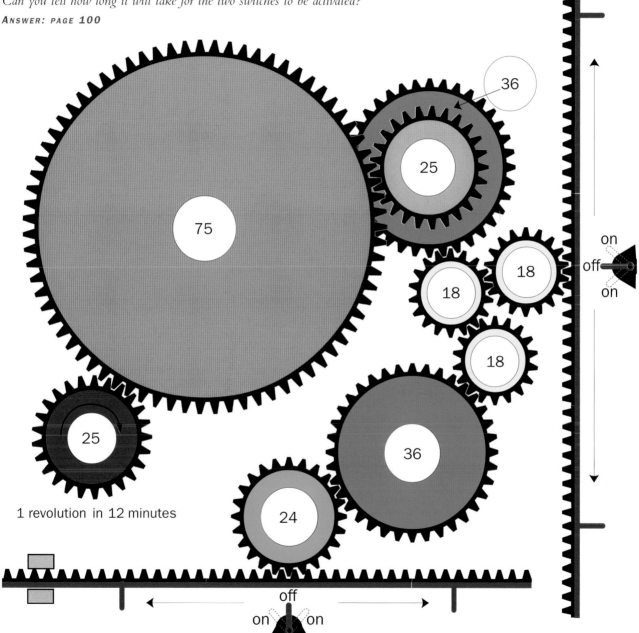

1 revolution in 12 minutes

▲ GEAR PUZZLE

How can you change the positions of the nine meshed gears so that there are matching colors along each of the 12 touching points?

ANSWER: PAGE 100

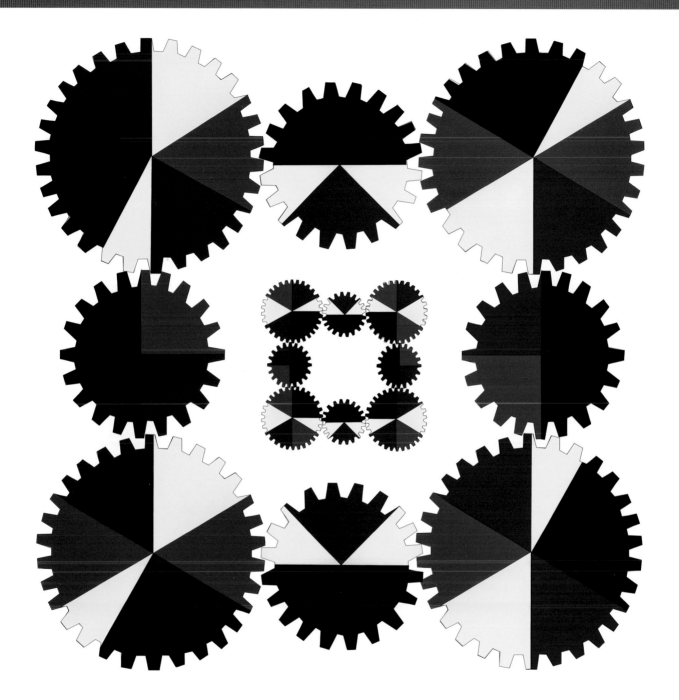

▲ GEAR SQUARE

How many times would you have to turn one of the small gears to form a black square in the circle of 8 meshed gears, as seen in the small center diagram?

The small gears have 20 teeth. The large gears have 30 teeth.

ANSWER: PAGE 101

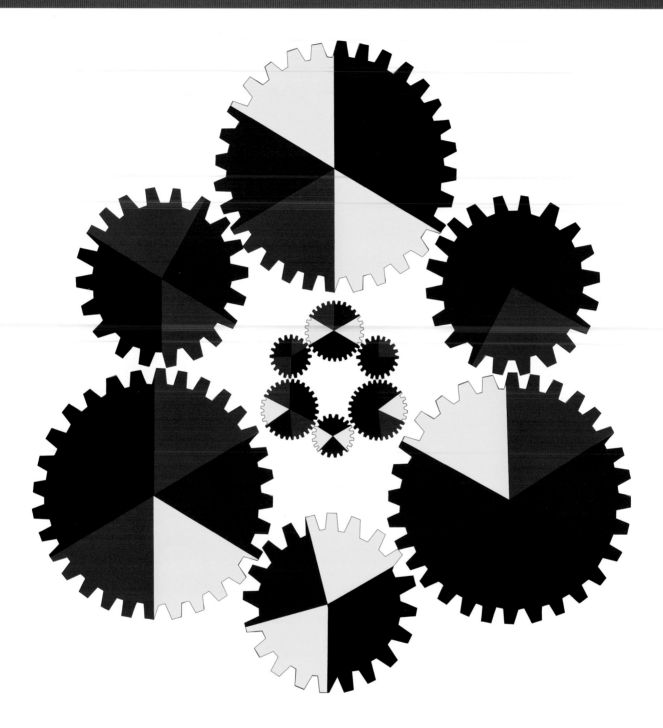

▲ GEAR HEXAGON

How much would you have to revolve one of the large gears to create a black hexagon shape in the inside of the six meshed gears, as seen in the small center diagram?

The large gears have 30 teeth, and the small gears have 20 teeth.

ANSWER: PAGE **101**

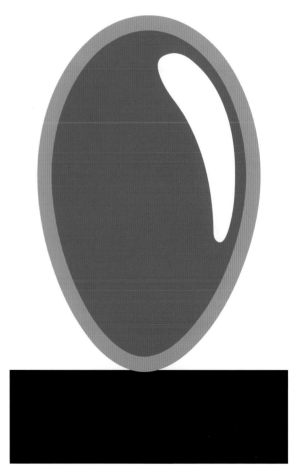

▲ THE COLUMBUS EGG

There is a famous problem: how can you stand an egg on its end? According to legend, Christpher Columbus knew how.

The story goes that Columbus was posed a problem by Spanish courtiers, which, according to them, was too difficult to solve.

Columbus's response was to challenge them to stand an egg on its thinner end. When all their attempts failed, Columbus took the egg, lightly cracked the shell at its thinner end and easily stood it on its end. The story is an example of how something that looks difficult may have a solution that seems quite obvious once it is pointed out.

Can you find another solution that accomplishes the same feat without damaging the egg?

ANSWER: PAGE 101

Building a structure with building blocks might seem like child's play, but getting the structure to stand up in the way we have shown is another story. How can it be done without the whole thing toppling over?

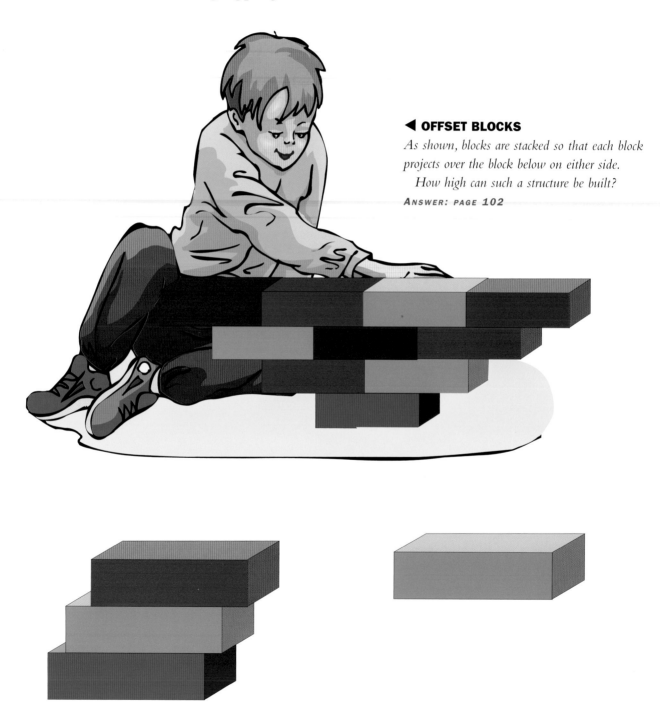

◀ **OFFSET BLOCKS**

As shown, blocks are stacked so that each block projects over the block below on either side.

How high can such a structure be built?

ANSWER: PAGE 102

▶ **CHANCE BALANCE**

How many ways can you find to arrange the five weights so that the scale is in equilibrium? Remember that the farther a weight is from the fulcrum, the more force it exerts. So a weight over the number 2 on the scale would exert twice as much force as the same weight over the number 1.

If you place the weights at random on the scale, what is the probability that they will be in equilibrium?

ANSWER: PAGE **102**

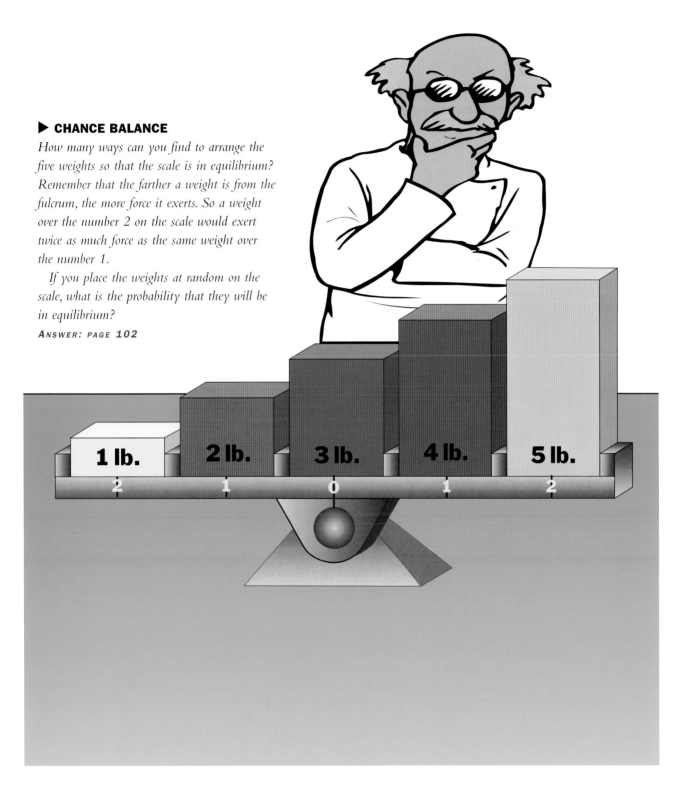

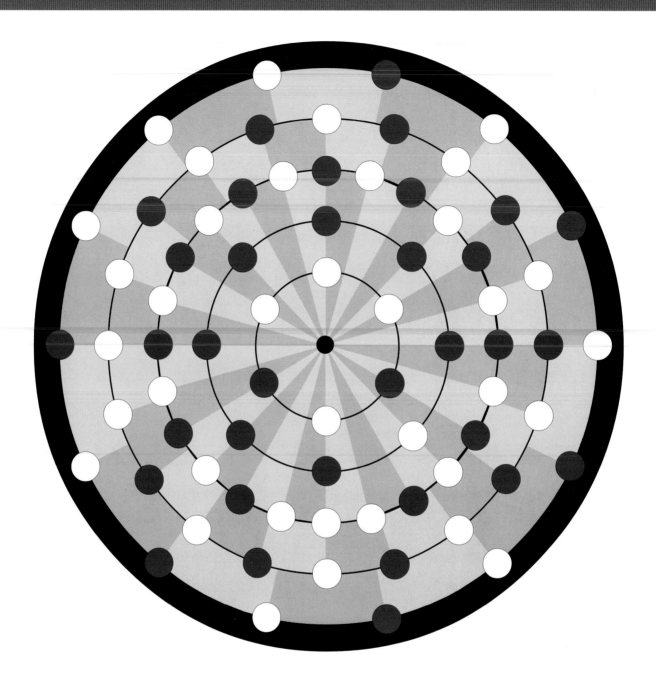

▲ BALANCING PLATFORM

Balancing platforms, often seen at children's playgrounds, can be a lot of fun. Here is a puzzle based on the same idea.

Equal weights (represented by red circles) are placed on some of the empty fields (white circles).

How many additional weights have to be placed and on which empty fields to achieve equilibrium if the platform has its fulcrum at the center (black point)?

ANSWER: PAGE 103

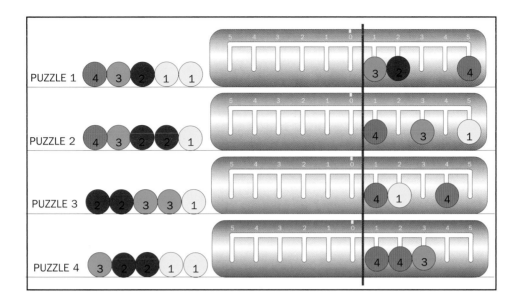

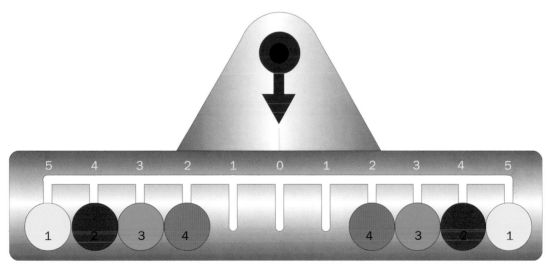

▲ MENTAL IMBALANCE

Eight sliding weights are enclosed in a frame as shown above and they can be moved into one of the 11 equally spaced slots. There are four different weights:

     yellow: 1 unit weight

     red: 2 unit weight

     green: 3 unit weight

     blue: 4 unit weight

In each of the four puzzles above, three weights have been fixed on the right side of the frame. The rest of the weights are to be distributed on the left side on the frame (including the middle slot) to create equilibrium. Placing a weight to the right of the red line is not permitted.

ANSWER: PAGE 104

Roman mosaics were made up of *tesserae*, small geometric shapes laid together which made up a complex pattern or picture. Today the term tessellation is used to describe any pattern of shapes that completely covers a surface.

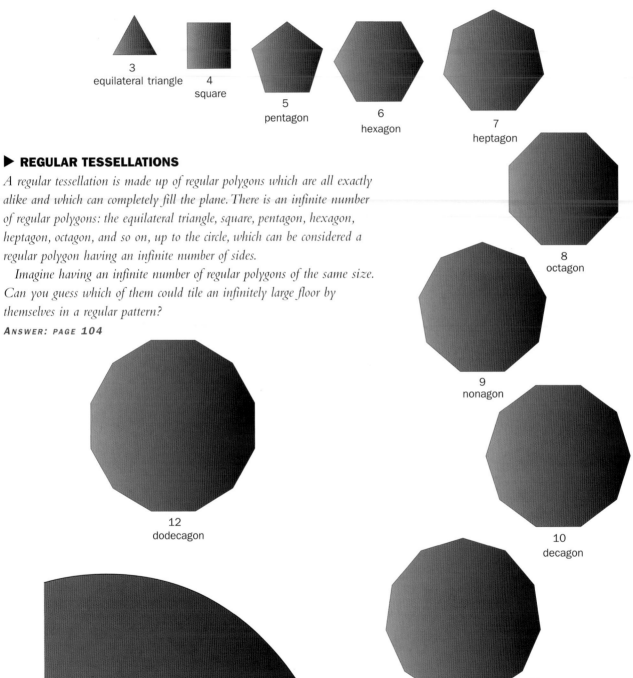

3
equilateral triangle

4
square

5
pentagon

6
hexagon

7
heptagon

8
octagon

9
nonagon

10
decagon

11
undecagon

12
dodecagon

▶ REGULAR TESSELLATIONS

A regular tessellation is made up of regular polygons which are all exactly alike and which can completely fill the plane. There is an infinite number of regular polygons: the equilateral triangle, square, pentagon, hexagon, heptagon, octagon, and so on, up to the circle, which can be considered a regular polygon having an infinite number of sides.

Imagine having an infinite number of regular polygons of the same size. Can you guess which of them could tile an infinitely large floor by themselves in a regular pattern?

ANSWER: PAGE **104**

▼ SEMIREGULAR TESSELLATIONS

Semiregular tessellations are those tessellations in which two or more kinds of regular polygons are fitted together to cover the plane in such a way that the same polygons, in the same relative positions, surround every vertex (corner point)—or, to put it in mathematical terms, so that every vertex is congruent to every other vertex.

Can you tell how many semiregular tessellations are possible? This information can be expressed using a simple notation as shown in the example, right. Here, {3, 3, 3, 3, 6} means that at every vertex there are four triangles and one hexagon in the same clockwise cyclic order.

In order to be able to answer this question a systematic procedure is needed. We have to find which combinations of regular polygons can fill the 360 degrees around a single vertex (the table on the right will help you work this out). Combinations of angles that can do this are called "vertex pictures." This is the basic condition to create any kind of tessellation, but it is not sufficient. Only some of these arrangements can be extended to tessellate the plane.

An example is given top right. Can you find seven others?

ANSWER: PAGE 105

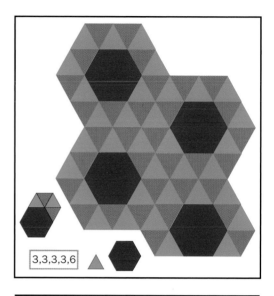

3,3,3,3,6

✳ Arranging geometric shapes

To tessellate means to arrange geometrical shapes to cover the plane in a mosaic pattern. Plane tessellations are the basic elements of the three-dimensional polyhedra. They are an important geometrical link between plane diagrams (polygons) and solid three-dimensional configurations. In fact, a plane tessellation is the special case of an infinite polyhedron.

ANGLES IN POLYGONS
The interior angles (in degrees) of regular polygons are, in general:

$$180(n - 2)/n$$

Number of sides	Interior angles
3	60
4	90
5	108
6	120
7	128.57
8	135
9	140
10	144
12	150
15	156
18	160
20	162
24	165
42	171.43

✳ Pinwheel patterns and triangles

A pattern in the plane has a symmetry of scale or is scalable if the tiles that make up the pattern can be grouped into super-tiles that cover the plane and, scaled down, coincide with the original pattern. Square patterns and patterns of equilateral triangles are examples.

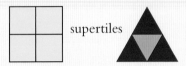
supertiles

Suppose we have a pattern that has a symmetry of scale. Must that pattern also have rigid symmetries? A rigid symmetry of a pattern in the plane is a motion of the plane that preserves the pattern without changing or distorting it.

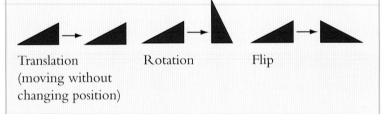

Translation
(moving without
changing position)

Rotation

Flip

A rigid symmetry could be a motion of a part of the pattern by a translation, rotation, a flip, or any combination of these. In the 1960s, Robert Berger at Harvard constructed patterns that had no rigid symmetries and yet had a scalable property. His examples used thousands of tiles.

An enormous development of this idea happened a decade later, with the discovery of Penrose patterns by Roger Penrose.

Penrose
patterns

They had no rigid symmetries and used only two tiles, called kites and darts. Penrose patterns are not completely chaotic since the two tiles can occur in one of only 10 possible orientations in a pattern.

In 1994, John Conway of Princeton University and Charles Radin of the University of Texas discovered another tiling: the pinwheel pattern, which uses only one single triangular tile and can occur in an infinite number of orientations in a tessellation. The pinwheel pattern has no rigid symmetries.

▼ PINWHEEL TRIANGLES AND SUPER-TILING

For a pattern to have a symmetry of scale, the basic requirement is to be able to group the tiles into super-tiles of the same shape as the original but larger. For the creation of pinwheel patterns the basic shape is the pinwheel triangle, a right-angled triangle with legs of lengths 1 and 2.

Five of such triangles form a super-tile called a 5-unit pinwheel triangle. There is only one way to group the pinwheel triangles into super-tiles to be able to create a pinwheel pattern in the plane, shown above.

Can you complete a 125-unit pinwheel triangle, or even a 625-unit triangle?

ANSWER: PAGE 106

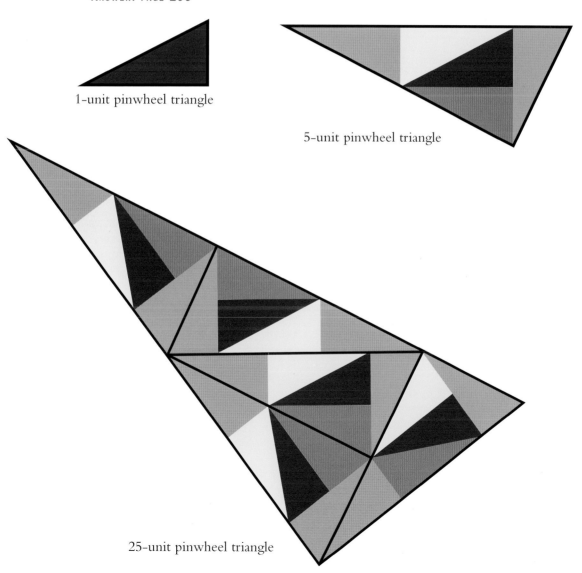

1–unit pinwheel triangle

5-unit pinwheel triangle

25-unit pinwheel triangle

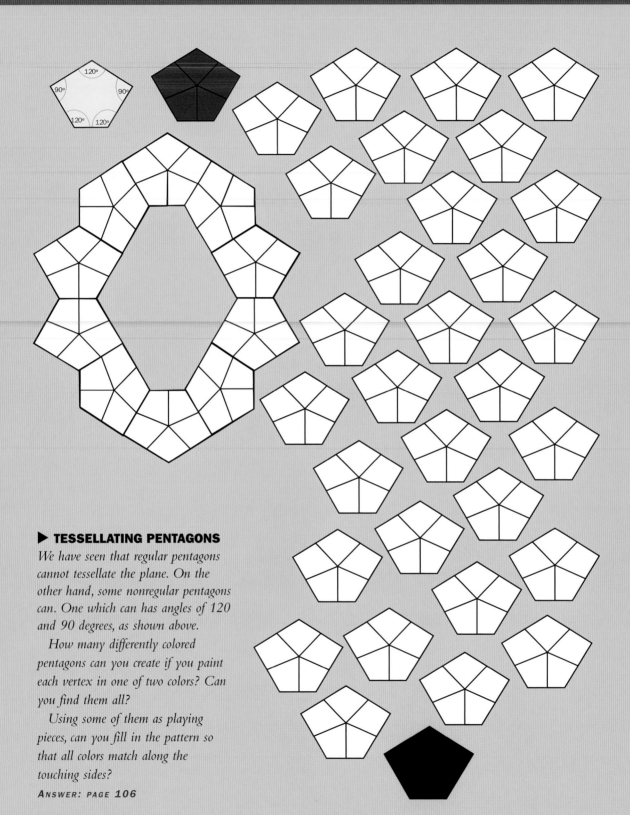

▶ TESSELLATING PENTAGONS

We have seen that regular pentagons cannot tessellate the plane. On the other hand, some nonregular pentagons can. One which can has angles of 120 and 90 degrees, as shown above.

How many differently colored pentagons can you create if you paint each vertex in one of two colors? Can you find them all?

Using some of them as playing pieces, can you fill in the pattern so that all colors match along the touching sides?

ANSWER: PAGE 106

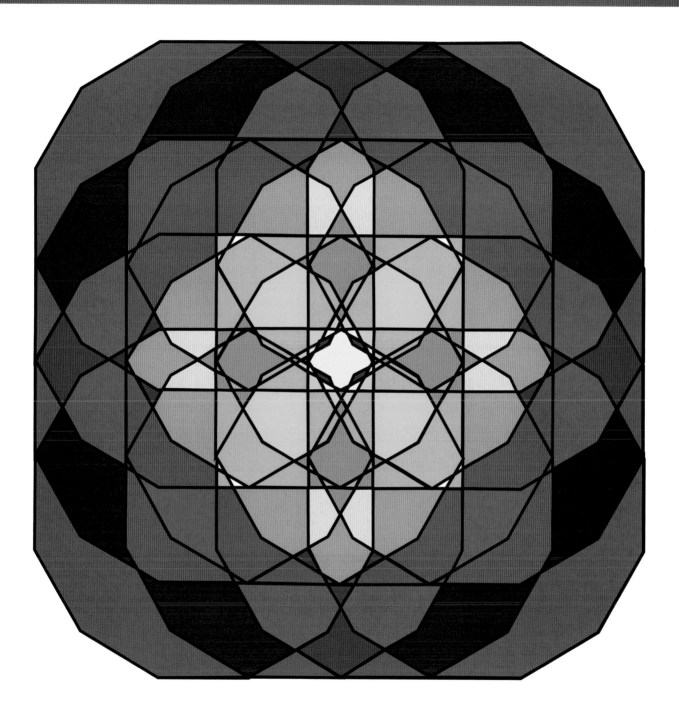

▲ OVERLAPPING TESSELLATION

The intricately colored tessellation, above, in which many irregular triangles, pentagons, hexagons, heptagons, and octagons can be found, was created from one single element.

Can you tell what it is?

ANSWER: PAGE 107

❋ Numbers

Natural numbers (that is, positive whole numbers) are useful for counting, but they are not sufficient even to solve a simple equation such as x + 2 = 0.

To solve such equations you need integers (both positive and negative whole numbers). Linear equations such as 2x + 3 = 0 need to include rationals (which include fractions).

For solving quadratic equations like $x^2 - 2 = 0$ rationals are not enough; you will need real numbers, which include irrational numbers. But even the realnumbers won't be sufficient to solve all quadratic equations, like $x^2 + 1 = 0$.

To solve this quadratic equation you have to employ complex numbers (which include imaginary numbers; imaginary numbers are the square roots of negative numbers). When you reach the complex numbers, the process comes to a halt. Any polynomial equation can be solved by the complex numbers. This important conclusion is known as the fundamental theorem of algebra.

The proof was provided by Gauss in his doctoral thesis in 1799.

Abacus vs. algorithms
Presiding over a contest between an abacist and an algorithmist—from the 16th-century book Margarita Philosophica by Gregor Reisch.

The abacist is calculating by means of an abacus, while the algorithmist uses written numerals. In some European countries calculating by "algorithm" was actually forbidden by law, and had to be done in secrecy.

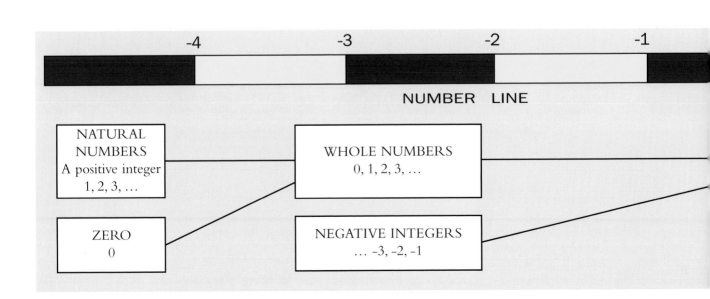

-4   -3   -2   -1

NUMBER LINE

| NATURAL NUMBERS |
| A positive integer |
| 1, 2, 3, … |

| WHOLE NUMBERS |
| 0, 1, 2, 3, … |

| ZERO |
| 0 |

| NEGATIVE INTEGERS |
| … –3, –2, –1 |

▼ NUMBER LINE

Since the numerals of the ancients were ill-adapted for purposes of calculation, some form of mechanical computation was necessary in the days before the introduction of the modern numerical system.

The ancient Egyptians used a decimal system: it had names and symbols for 10, 100, 1,000, 10,000, 100,000 and 1,000,000; however, it did not employ the principle of position or use a zero.

So the counting frame or abacus appeared about 5,000 years ago. It was a primitive but effective digital computer— a mathematical toy, still in use today. It is one of those rare inventions that is so simple yet so effective that it was passed on unchanged from civilization to civilization. Long before the concept of zero was invented the abacus used an empty column as part of its computations.

The ancient Greeks used the entire alphabet as symbols representing numbers. In a similar fashion the Roman system used specific letters and letter combinations to represent numbers. The appearance of the first zero was on a Babylonian clay tablet around 200 B.C. Rational numbers (including fractions) appear as early as 1500 B.C. in the Rhind Papyrus of ancient Egypt. In the 6th century B.C., the Pythagoreans encountered a number—√2—that could not be fitted into existing categories. Their discovery was tantamount to finding that the diagonal of a square did not have a measurable length.

The question still remains: was the first irrational number √2 (resulting from applying the Pythagorean theorem to a right triangle with legs of 1 unit); phi (1+√5)/2, the golden ratio (derived from the use of the golden rectangle); or pi (the ratio between the circumference and diameter in a circle)?

Negative numbers were fully incorporated into mathematics in 1545, with the publication of Girolamo Cardano's Ars Magna.

The Hindus of India during the early centuries of the Christian era formulated the principle of position and the use of ten symbols to represent zero and the first nine digits. Though the advantages of this system were obvious, it was not until the 13th century that it reached Western Europe (by way of Arabia), and its adoption took several centuries.

Can all the real numbers be found on the number line?

ANSWER: PAGE 108

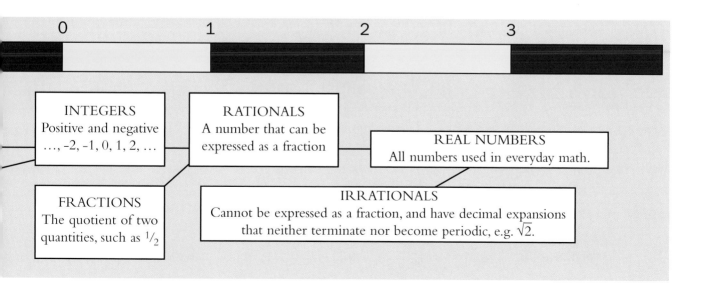

INTEGERS
Positive and negative
..., -2, -1, 0, 1, 2, ...

RATIONALS
A number that can be expressed as a fraction

REAL NUMBERS
All numbers used in everyday math.

FRACTIONS
The quotient of two quantities, such as $\frac{1}{2}$

IRRATIONALS
Cannot be expressed as a fraction, and have decimal expansions that neither terminate nor become periodic, e.g. √2.

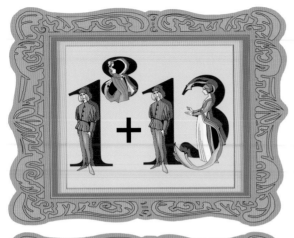

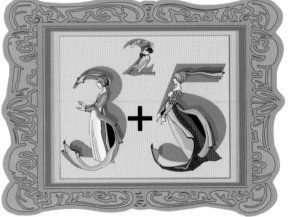

▲ GALLERY OF NUMBERS

For the ancient Greeks, numbers were everything, so in our gallery numbers are works of art.

Some art experts like evenism (even-numbered art), while others like oddism (odd-numbered art).

Connoisseurs can tell just by looking which paintings are evenistic and which are oddistic. Can you?

ANSWER: PAGE **108**

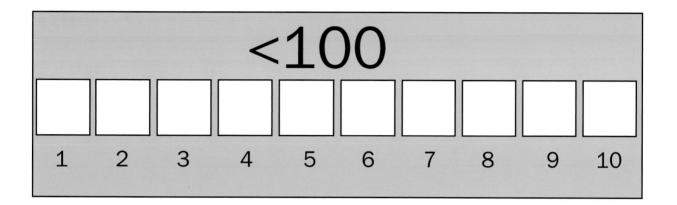

▲ NUMBER SELECTION

Select 10 different positive numbers smaller than 100. Find two sets of numbers from your selection which add up to the same total. Each set can contain one or more numbers, but the same number cannot appear in both sets. Can you always achieve this?

For example:

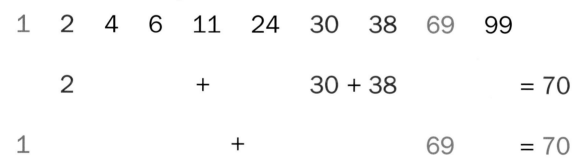

ANSWER: PAGE 108

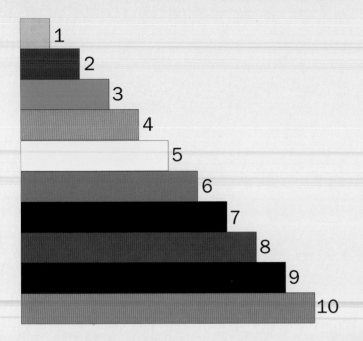

✳ Cuisenaire number rods

Simple rods with consecutive lengths from 1 to 10 units, Cuisenaire number rods can be ideal tools for teaching basic arithmetic. They were devised about 60 years ago by the Belgian mathematics teacher Emile Cuisenaire.

▶ **SUMS TO TEN**

Using one set of rods we can demonstrate several ways to combine them to add up to 10.

Using an unlimited number of Cuisenaire rods we can combine them to add up to 10 in many more ways.

How many?

ANSWER: PAGE 109

10

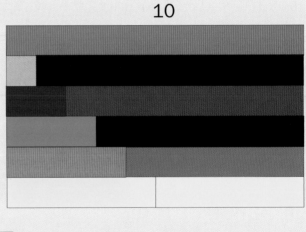

◀ **CUISENAIRE PUZZLE**

Using one set of rods, can you fill the outline?

ANSWER: PAGE 109

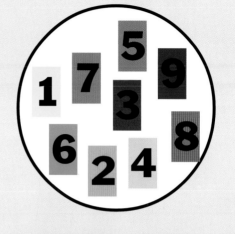

$$? ? ? ? ? ? ? ? \times 6 = ? ? ? ? ? ? ? ? ?$$

✳ Number sequences

Throughout history, numbers have been believed to hold powers that could enlist help from spirits, perform witchcraft, and predict the end of the world. Numerological mystics wove ingenious number patterns to explain anything and everything. To the ancients, numbers revealed the patterns of the universe. Nature is mathematics.

Usually numbers are considered as individual entities, but there is another way numbers can be presented. We may consider a succession of numbers and observe the tendencies of their succession as a whole. By treating numbers as structures this way, interesting patterns and conclusions can be derived.

The simplest kind of pattern is a sequence. A number sequence is a list of numbers that follows a certain pattern, the most simple number sequence being 1, 2, 3, 4, 5…

A number series is different: it is the sum of numbers in a sequence. For instance, the series $1 + \frac{1}{2} + \frac{1}{4} + \frac{1}{8} + \frac{1}{16}…$ has a limit (the sum that the series would total if continued indefinitely) of 2.

Some number sequences, such as the arithmetic progressions 1, 2, 3, 4… and 1, 3, 5, 7… are simple enough, while others can be less obvious. To see what comes next in a sequence you have to understand the pattern by which it is organized.

▲ DIGITS 1 TO 9

Arrange the digits 1, 2, 3, 4, 5, 7, 8, and 9 so that when they are multiplied by 6, the product will contain each of the nine digits exactly once.

ANSWER: PAGE 109

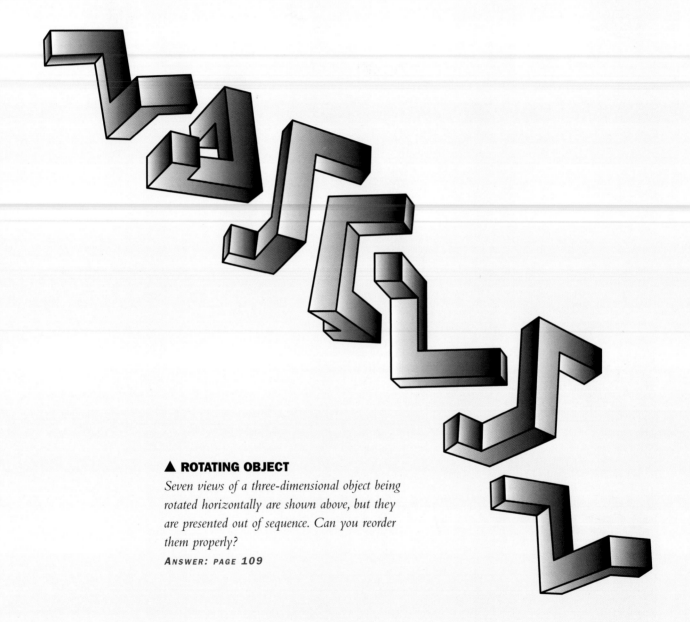

▲ ROTATING OBJECT

Seven views of a three-dimensional object being rotated horizontally are shown above, but they are presented out of sequence. Can you reorder them properly?

ANSWER: PAGE 109

▲ ORBITAL ILLUSION

Johannes Kepler (1571–1630) discovered that planets travel around the sun in elliptical orbit. Is the planet shown above orbiting in an ellipse?

ANSWER: PAGE 109

Ancient Greek arithmetic was occupied with studying figurate numbers, the study of which led to the study of number series. Here we will have a look at figurate and triangular numbers

❋ Figurate numbers

If whole numbers are represented by dots or disks arranged in certain geometric shapes, they can form groups or series called polygonal or figurate numbers. Figurate numbers can provide intuitive insights into many aspects of elementary number theory.

The visual representation of figurate numbers can often offer an elegant proof of a theorem that can be seen and understood at a glance. A method for finding the sum of the first n natural numbers can be visualized with "triangular numbers"; the sum of consecutive odd integers can be shown with square numbers; etc.

❋ Triangular numbers

Triangular numbers can be found by stacking a group of objects in a triangular fashion—two objects are placed after one, three objects after two, and so on.

The fourth triangular number, for example, is 10: 1 + 2 + 3 + 4 = 10, as shown.

Triangular numbers represent the sum of a number of consecutive integers.

You won't have a very difficult time counting the tenth triangular number, shown below. But how long will it take you to find the hundredth triangular number?

When Karl Friedrich Gauss (1777–1855), the famous German mathematician, was six years old, he found it in seconds!

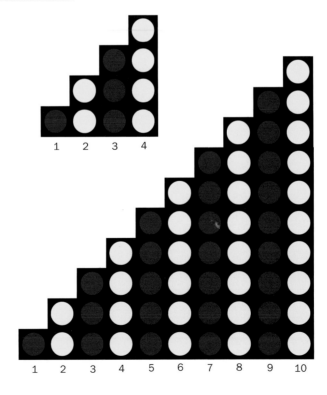

▼ PLAYING THE TRIANGLE

The 100th triangular number is shown below. How long will it take you to count the dots? How did Gauss do it?

ANSWER: PAGE 110

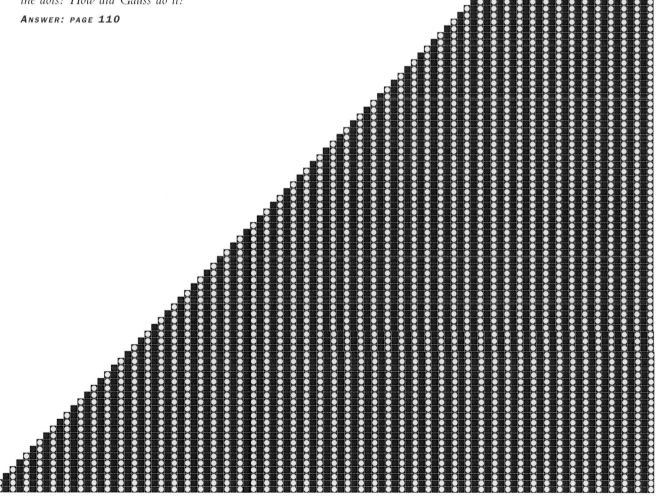

▼ THREE-DIMENSIONAL FIGURATE NUMBERS

Three-dimensional analogs of plane figurate numbers are obtained by packing spheres in three-sided pyramids (which form the tetrahedral numbers), and four-sided pyramids (representing the pyramidal numbers).

The tetrahedral numbers begin: 1, 4, 10…. The differences between numbers in the series are the triangular numbers

The pyramidal numbers begin: 1, 5, 14…. The differences between numbers in the series are the square numbers. The first three numbers of each series have been given. Can you continue both series to the seventh number?

The square pyramid is built up of identical spheres. How many balls will be in the bottom (tenth) layer of the pyramid? How many spheres are in the whole pyramid?

ANSWER: PAGE 110

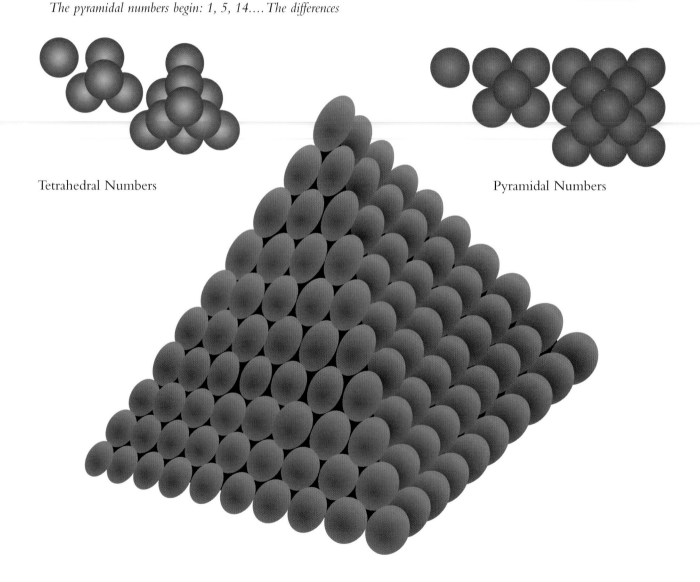

Tetrahedral Numbers

Pyramidal Numbers

$$\frac{\frac{1}{4} \quad \frac{1}{5} \quad \frac{1}{6}}{\$37}$$

▲ PIGGY BANK

One fourth, one fifth, and one sixth of my savings added together make $37.

How much money did I save?

ANSWER: PAGE **110**

Word puzzles and paradoxes

Yogi Berra is almost as famous for the things he's said as for his talent on the baseball field. His twists of logic are actually known as Yogi-isms:"No one goes to that restaurant anymore—it's too crowded"; "A nickel ain't worth a dime anymore"; "If you come to a fork in the road, take it."

What is funny and ultimately lovely about Berra's speech is its paradoxical nature. We know what he meant, but if we examine what he actually said, we realize that his statements are contradictions. Their internal logic breaks down.

Words are much more flexible than numbers, so the rules concerning language are usually more flexible than the rules of mathematics. Contradictions are allowed, even encouraged, in wordplay, but "Two plus two equals seven" won't get a laugh out of anyone.

Logic—the study of ideas and how they are used in argument—is much more rigid, much more like math than language. At its essence, logic governs the form of an argument rather than the accuracy of its facts.

The ancient Greeks, notably Aristotle, were the first to apply logical processes to statements such as syllogisms, which are arguments in three parts: two premises, on which the argument is based, and one conclusion. Strict rules govern what makes a syllogism valid.

Centuries later Gottfried Wilhelm Leibniz, the 17th-century German philosopher and mathematician, suggested that logic could be organized in terms of a mathematical language such as algebra. The 19th-century British mathematician George Boole finally linked logic with mathematics and devised such a language: premises and conclusions are represented by algebraic symbols and are linked by other symbols to form a logical argument. When scientists today are confronted by a problem, they then work out the answer using the language of Boolean logic.

Mathematicians sometimes find a mathematical paradox—a conclusion so unexpected that it is difficult to accept even though every step in reasoning is known to be valid.

A mathematical fallacy, on the other hand, is an instance of improper reasoning leading to an unexpected result that is patently false or absurd.

When mathematicians—or any of us—stumble across such a fallacy, there is a moment of genuine surprise at the fact that logical arguments can lead to quite unreasonable conclusions.

But the feeling rarely lasts long. Faith in intuition as a guide to what is and what is not possible is very strong, and we soon turn our attention to finding the flaw in the argument. When there is a flaw, tracking it down can be enjoyable and challenging. But there are many cases in which the logical consequences of reasonable premises are not so reasonable and sometimes downright unbelievable: At times like that, we must accept that our intuition often is a poor guide.

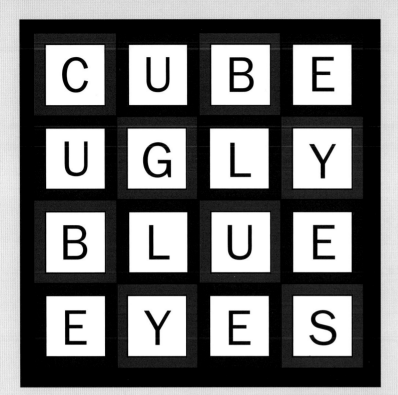

◄ WORD SQUARES

Word squares are square matrices in which each word appears twice, once horizontally and once vertically, as shown in the order-4 word square, at left.

The higher the order, the more difficult it is to devise such squares. Try to complete the order-5 square below.

ANSWER: PAGE 110

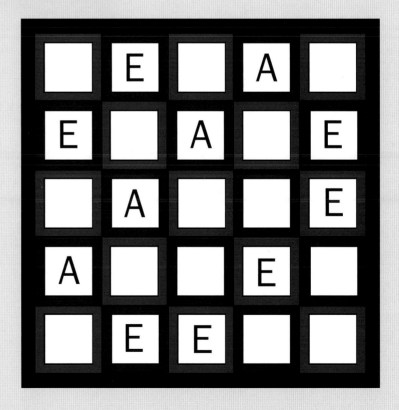

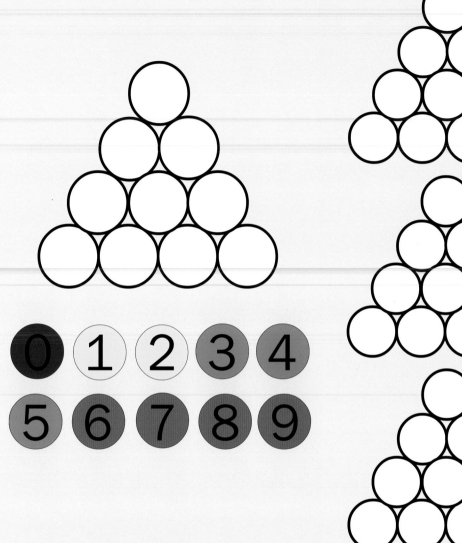

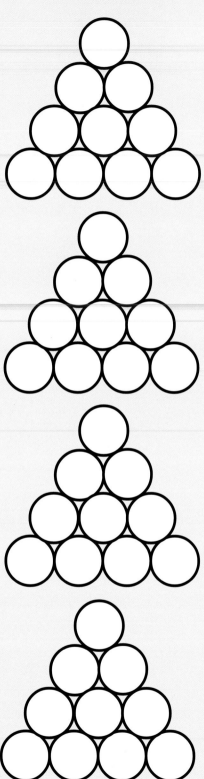

▲ TRIANGULAR NUMBERS

Can you arrange the first ten digits (including zero) in the triangular configuration so that the sums on its three sides are equal?

How many different arrangements can you find?

ANSWER: PAGE 111

First centered
hexagonal number

Second centered
hexagonal number

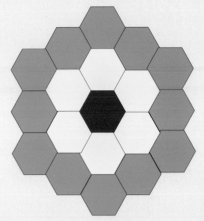

Third centered
hexagonal number

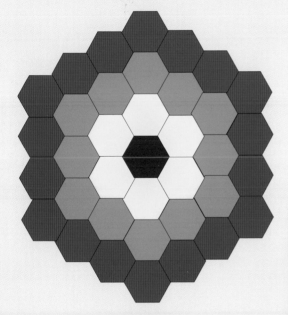

Fourth centered
hexagonal number

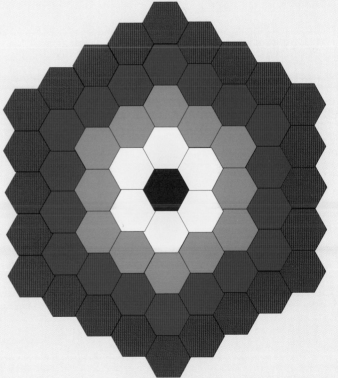

Fifth centered
hexagonal number

▲ CENTERED HEXAGONAL NUMBERS

*The first five centered hexagonal figurate numbers are
depicted above. They are "centered" because they build
outwards from a central core.*

1) *Can you determine the sixth hexagonal number?*
2) *Can you work out the sum of the first 6
   hexagonal numbers?*
3) *Can you work out the general formula for
   both cases?*

ANSWER: PAGE 112

The Greeks got a big shock when they discovered that the diagonal of a square with rational sides does not have a rational length.

God made the integers: all the rest is the work of man.
Leopold Kronecker

▼ IRRATIONAL

Is it possible to construct a triangle with one right angle, two identical sides, and with the hypotenuse being a natural number?

The ancient Greeks assumed that any length or area is rational, i.e., that it could be expressed by a natural number (a whole number or a fraction of two whole numbers). Rational numbers can be expressed as quotients of two whole numbers 'a/b'; irrational numbers can't.

The Pythagoreans preoccupation with right-angled triangles led them to measure the diagonal of a square of unit side. They knew how to do that using a compass and a straight edge. But could they express this length as a natural number? The discovery that they could not came as an immense shock to the Greek mathematician Hippasus, a Pythagorean who showed that the diagonal of a square with rational sides does not have a rational length. The proof of this fact depends on the Pythagorean theorem, and after this discovery, the universe that the Pythagoreans had built on rational numbers came tumbling down.

Can you figure out how Hippasus proved that a unit square's diagonal has an irrational length?

ANSWER: PAGE 113

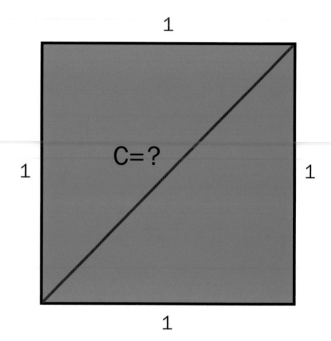

1

1   C=?   1

1

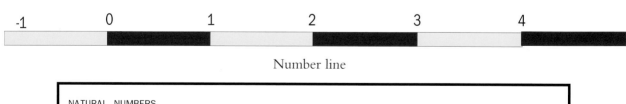

Number line

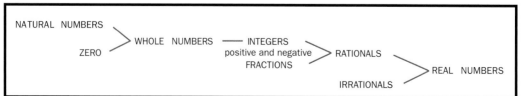

▶ ADDITION

Cross out nine digits in the addition problem at right so that the total of the remaining numbers will be 1,111.

ANSWER: PAGE 113

```
  1 1 1
  3 3 3
  5 5 5
  7 7 7
+ 9 9 9
_____
  1 1 1 1
```

```
    8
    8
    8
    8
    8
    8
    8
  + 8
_____
  1000
```

▶ EIGHT EIGHTS

Arrange eight eights in such a way that they will add up to 1,000.

ANSWER: PAGE 113

7356432633183741

▲ ADD UP TO 15

How many groups of consecutive digits in the above line add up to 15?

ANSWER: PAGE 113

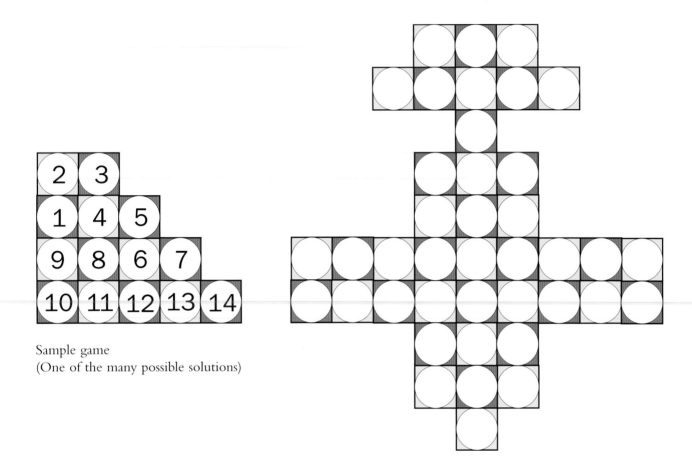

Sample game
(One of the many possible solutions)

▲ HIROIMONO

This game originated in 14th-century Japan and is played by arranging stones in an orthogonal pattern and removing them one by one, according to the rules of the game. It can also be played as a paper-and-pencil game by filling the patterns with consecutive numbers starting from 1, as shown in the sample game at above left.

The object is to fill all circles of the given pattern with consecutive numbers, starting at a chosen circle.

The rules are:

1) Once you have written a number in a circle, you may move horizontally or vertically to the next empty circle in that direction.

2) You may not jump over an empty circle, but you may jump filled circles to reach an empty circle.

3) You may not land on a circle you have previously visited.

Can you solve the given puzzle?

▼ DIVISIBILITY

What is the smallest number divisible by all of the following?

1,   2,   3,   4,   5,   6,   7,   8,   and   9?

ANSWER: PAGE 114

348,926,128

845,386,720

457,873,804

567,467,334

895,623,724

◄ DIVISIBILITY AGAIN

Just by looking at the five numbers, can you tell which are divisible by 4 and by 8?

ANSWER: PAGE 114

35 = ? + ? + ? + ?

48 = ? + ? + ? + ?

▲ LAGRANGE'S THEOREM

Every whole number is the sum of no more than four squares, or, to put it another way, any rectangular surface whose area is a whole number can be broken into up to four surfaces whose areas are squares of whole numbers, (although the borders of the areas do not have to be squares).

Can you find the component squares for the two numbers?

ANSWER: PAGE 114

Top-left grid (4×4):

	7		
	1		

Top-right grid (4×4, example):

6	7	8	9
5	4	3	10
16	1	2	11
15	14	13	12

Bottom-left grid (5×5):

5			24	
				20
	9	16		14

Bottom-right grid (6×6):

15					
					1
			10		
	20				
				32	

▲ NUMBER LABYRINTHS

*A number labyrinth for a square grid of side
n is a continuous sequence of numbers from
1 to n² moving horizontally or vertically through
adjacent cells, with one number occupying each
cell. An example is shown above.*

*In the 5-by-5 and 6-by-6 grids some cells
already have numbers in them. Can you
complete the number paths?*

ANSWER: PAGE 115

▼ BIG LABYRINTH

Here's another number labyrinth. It works just like the ones on the previous page, but the numbers go from 1 to 100.

Can you complete the number path?

ANSWER: PAGE 115

	100							69	
	87				77				
13		29							60
							23		
								38	
	46								
							1		

Although these two puzzles use only a limited number of digits, getting them all placed within the framework of each puzzle is tricky. Give it a try!

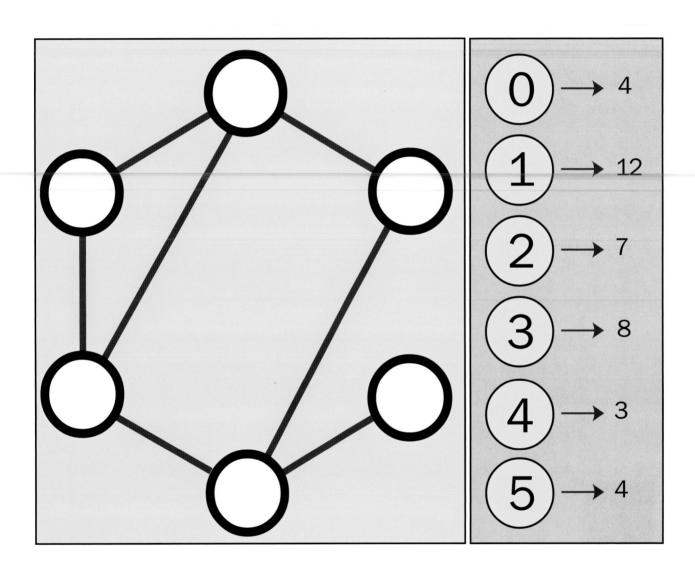

▲ **NUMBER NEIGHBORS 1**

Can you place the numbers from 0 to 5 in the circles of the gameboard so that the sum of each number's neighbors (the numbers they are connected to with a red line) are as shown?

ANSWER: PAGE 116

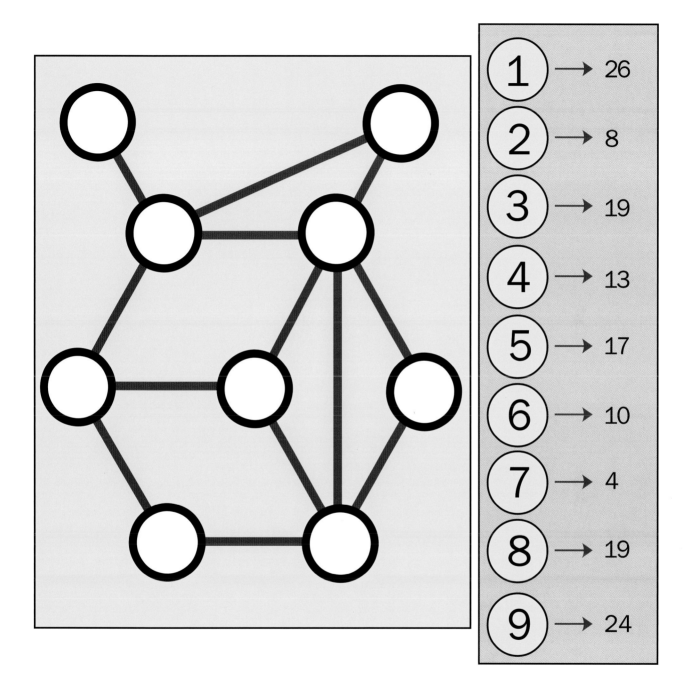

▲ **NUMBER NEIGHBORS 2**

Can you place the numbers from 1 to 9 in the circles of the gameboard so that the sums of each number's neighbors are as shown?

ANSWER: PAGE 116

◄ NUMBER SUMS AND DIFFERENCES

Can you rearrange the ten numbers in a row so that each number (except the first and the last) is the sum or difference of its two neighbors?

ANSWER: PAGE 116

2 3 5 6 7 8

10 11 12 13 14

15 17 18 19

20 21 22 23

24 26 27... ?

▲ **NUMBER SEQUENCE**

Can you explain the number sequence and continue it further?

ANSWER: PAGE 116

▲ SELF-DESCRIPTIVE NUMBER

In the Ontario Science Center in Toronto, an intriguing puzzle can be found in the mathematics exhibit. The object is to write a ten-digit number in the ten empty boxes of the second row according to the following rule:

The first digit indicates the total number of zeros in the ten-digit number; the second digit the total number of ones; the third digit the total number of twos; and so on until the last digit, which indicates the total number of nines.

The result is like a ten-digit number inventing itself. No wonder Martin Gardner called it a self-descriptive number.

How can one solve such a challenging problem? Is there a solution at all?

Daniel Shoham from MIT discovered some insights that help one approach the problem. He concluded that because there are ten different digits in row 1, the sum of the digits in row 2 must be 10 and determined the maximum number of possible values for each digit of the number in the second row.

Can you follow his logic and find the unique solution to the puzzle?

ANSWER: PAGE 117

▲ KAPREKAR'S MAGIC

Choose any four-digit number with four different digits—for example, 2435.

Rearrange the digits in descending order (in this case, 5432) and subtract from that the number you get when the digits are placed in ascending order:

5432 − 2345.

Do the same thing with the number you get as a result, and continue doing this until you get the same answer twice in a row.

I have a prediction as to what that number is. Turn to the answer section to see if I'm right!

ANSWER: PAGE 118

▲ CARDS AROUND

Fifteen cards are distributed around the table. Two cards have been turned facing up, as shown.

Each set of three adjacent cards adds up to 21.

Can you work out the value of each card?

ANSWER: PAGE **118**

▼ CALCULATOR TROUBLE

Calculators are usually reliable, but I have an old one on which none of the keys work except for the 1, 2, and 3.

Using just these three keys (1, 2, and 3), how many different one-, two-, and three-digit numbers can you make on this calculator?

ANSWER: PAGE 119

0,1,2,3,4,5,6,7,8,9,11,22,33,44,55,66,77,88,99,101,111,121,...?

▲ PALINDROMES

Words aren't the only things that can be palindromic.

Take any positive number, reverse its digits, and add them to the original number. Repeat this procedure with the sum you get until you end up with a palindromic number, as we have done below with 234, 1,924, and 5,280:

234	1924	5280
+432	+4291	+0825
666	6215	6105
	+5126	+5016
	11341	11121
	+14311	+12111
	25652	23232

89

▪ ▪ ▪ ▪

▪ ▪ ▪ ▪

▪ ▪ ?

Will every number ultimately produce a palindromic number with this procedure? Try 89 and see how that goes!

ANSWER: PAGE 119

Many interesting and challenging mathematical puzzles have been devised using the common functions of adding, subtracting, multiplying, and dividing. This puzzle makes use of all four.

▶ FOUR FOURS

Martin Gardner once featured this challenging puzzle in his "Mathematical Games" column.

The object of the game is to express as many whole numbers as possible, using the digit 4 exactly four times—no more, no less—in equations with common mathematical functions: addition, subtraction, multiplication, and division. You can also use parentheses.

For example:

$1 = {}^{44}/_{44}$

$2 = \frac{4}{4} + \frac{4}{4}$

It is possible to construct every digit from 1 to 10 this way.

If square roots are also allowed, you can make the numbers from 11 through 20, with one exception.

Can you find the equations for the numbers from 3 to 20, and find the number that can't be expressed this way? (There is a way to express it, but it involves a different mathematical function—can you figure it out?)

ANSWER: PAGE 119

$$1 = {}^{44}\!/_{44}$$

$$2 = \frac{4}{4} + \frac{4}{4}$$

$$3 =$$

$$4 =$$

$$5 =$$

$$6 =$$

$$7 =$$

$$8 =$$

$$9 =$$

$$10 =$$

$$11 =$$

$$12 =$$

$$13 =$$

$$14 =$$

$$15 =$$

$$16 =$$

$$17 =$$

$$18 =$$

$$19 =$$

$$20 =$$

▲ FOUR-DIGIT MUTANTS

Did I tell you about the mutant aliens who knew only four digits—1, 2, 3, and 4.

How many one-, two-, three-, and four-digit numbers could they make using only these four digits?

ANSWER: PAGE 120

▲ NUMBER SEQUENCE

Can you continue the number sequence above?
If you do, as a reward you will get the missing piece of cake!

ANSWER: PAGE 120

▲ SOCCER BALL

If the soccer ball weighs 5 ounces plus three quarters of its own weight, how much does the soccer ball weigh?

ANSWER: PAGE 120

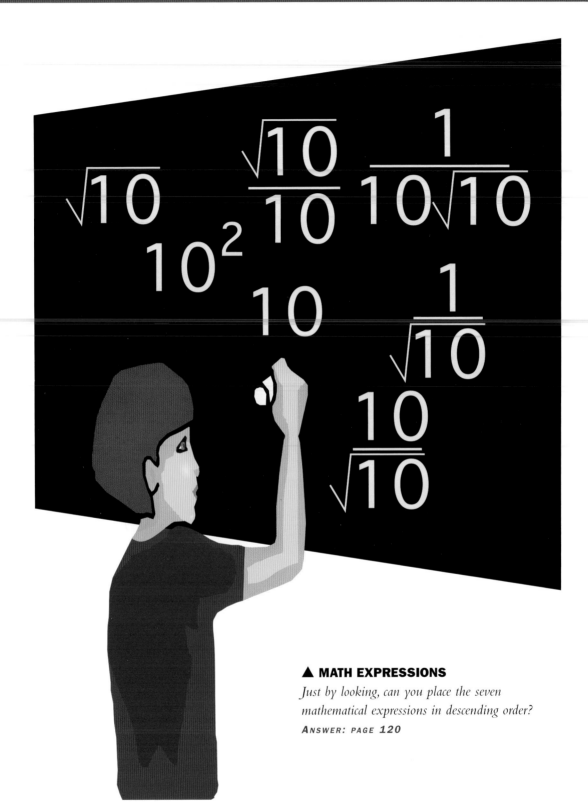

▲ **MATH EXPRESSIONS**

Just by looking, can you place the seven mathematical expressions in descending order?

ANSWER: PAGE 120

▲ HALF OF ELEVEN

Can you find a way in which six is half of eleven?

ANSWER: PAGE 121

$$6 + 6 = 11$$

▼ ADD A LINE

Add just one line to make the equation true.

ANSWER: PAGE 121

$$5 + 5 + 5 = 550$$

▼ THINK OF A NUMBER

Think of a number.
Add 10.
Double the result.
Subtract 6.
Divide by 2 and take away the number you originally thought of.
The result will always be 7.
Why?

ANSWER: PAGE 121

GENERATION	NUMBER SEQUENCE
1	1
2	11
3	21
4	1211
5	111221
6	312211
7	13112221
8	1113213211
9	?
10	?

▲ **THE LIKENESS SEQUENCE**

Eight consecutive generations of an interesting number sequence are shown above.

Can you figure out the logic and find the ninth and tenth generations?

ANSWER: PAGE 122

▲ HAILSTONE NUMBERS

Think of a number. If it is odd, triple it and add one. If it is even, halve it.

Continue applying these rules over and over to each number so obtained. For example:

1, 4, 2, 1, 4, 2, 1, 4, 2, 1, 4, 2...

2, 1, 4, 2, 1, 4, 2, 1, 4, 2...

3, 10, 5, 16, 8, 4, 2, 1, 4, 2...

As we can see, all the above sequences quickly end with the same loop.

Will all number sequences, regardless of the starting numbers, eventually end up in the same endless loop?

Try starting the sequence with 7 and a few other numbers before looking at the answer section for more information.

ANSWER: PAGE **122**

▲ PERSISTENCE OF NUMBERS

A number's "persistence" is the measure of how long it takes to be demolished down to a single digit by multiplying its digits together.

For instance, if we multiply the individual digits of the number 723 together—7 x 2 x 3—we get 42. Repeating this process we get 8. That took two steps, so 2 is the "persistence" for the number 723.

What are the smallest numbers that lead to persistence numbers of 2, 3, 4, 5, and so on?

Can you tell whether every starting number leads to a single digit in the end?

ANSWER: PAGE 122

▶ DIFFERENCE HEXAGONS

Can you fill in the proper numbers in the empty hexagons so that the number in each hexagon shows the sum of the two numbers in the two hexagons immediately above it? Negative numbers are not allowed!

ANSWER: PAGE 122

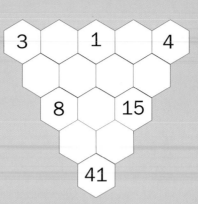

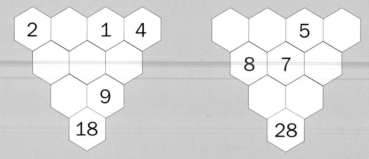

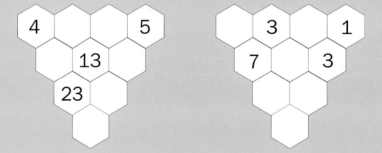

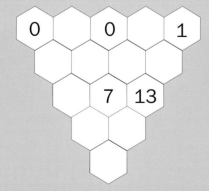

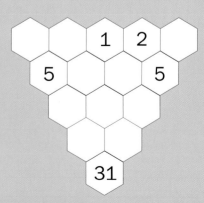

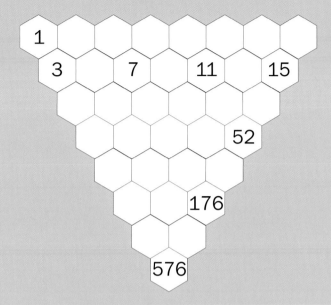

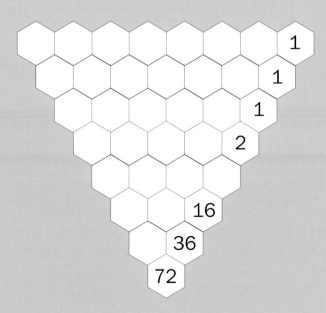

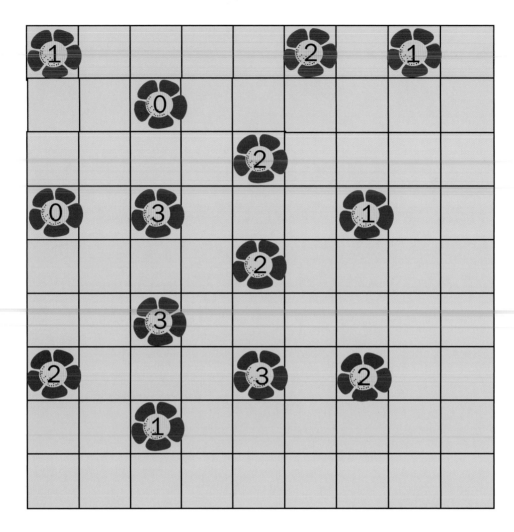

▲ LADYBUG GARDEN

Thirteen ladybugs are hiding among the squares of the garden and you must find them all.

The flowers on the grid all have numbers that indicate the number of ladybugs in that cell's eight neighboring squares (as in the example on the right).

Ladybugs cannot occupy any square that has a flower in it.

ANSWER: PAGE 124

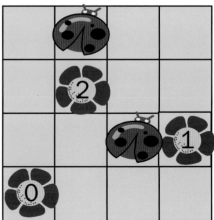

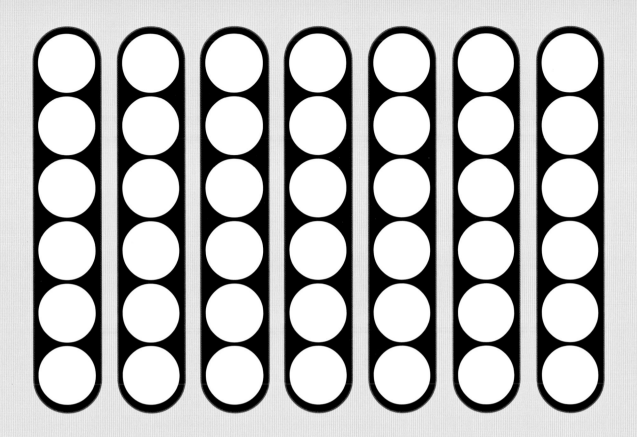

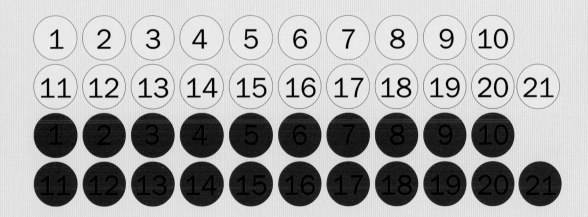

▲ NUMBER CARDS

Can you distribute the two sets of consecutive numbers from 1 to 21 on the seven number cards, so that every number appears on two cards and every pair of cards has exactly one number in common?

ANSWER: PAGE 124

These puzzles were created by C. Dudley Langford, a Scottish mathematician, as he watched his small son playing with a series of colored blocks. Can you tell who wins the race?

▶ RUNNING ORDER

There are four teams of runners with two runners in each team. We see them above, all starting a race simultaneously.

As they cross the finish line, one runner finishes between the red pair, two runners finish between the blue pair, three runners finish between the green pair, and, finally, four runners finish between the yellow pair.

We also know that a yellow runner finished last.

Can you tell what order the runners finished in (by color)?

ANSWER: PAGE 125

▲ RUNNING TRIPLETS

There are nine teams of runners, with three runners in each team. Each team wears uniforms with the same number. They crossed the finish line such that each team's second team member to finish was separated from his teammates by a number of other runners equal to his uniform number, as shown. The same principle applies to the other numbered teams. Given that a member of team 1 won the race, can you figure out how they all crossed the finish line?

ANSWER: PAGE 125

Team number 2's middle finisher is separated from his teammates by two runners on each side at the finish. (Note that these are not necessarily the places in which the members of team 2 finished.)

▲ CONSECUTIVE WEIGHTS

Puzzle 1) The scale holds three consecutive weights (weights which are of different but sequential whole-number weights) weighing a total of 54 grams. How much does each weigh?

Puzzle 2) The scale holds four consecutive weights weighing a total of 90 grams. How much does each weigh?

ANSWER: PAGE 125

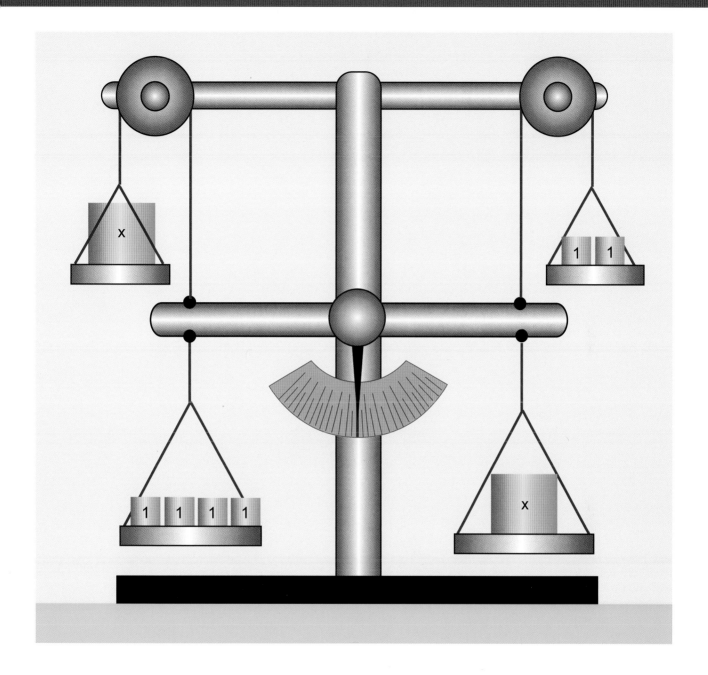

▲ EQUATION BALANCE

An equation may be likened to a scale. Robert Kitchen, a British schoolteacher, devised an ingenious scale that incorporates pulleys above a conventional scale, so that "negative weights" could be introduced, pulling upwards.

Can you express the above equilibrium situation as an equation, and determine the value of x?

ANSWER: PAGE 125

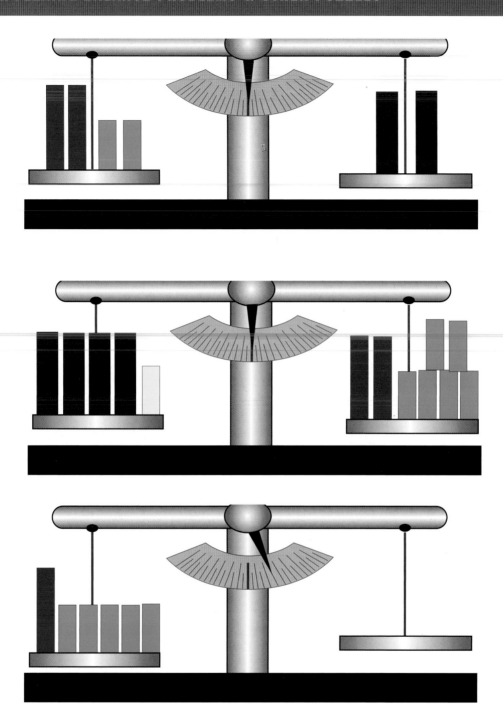

▲ WEIGHTY MATTERS 1

The two upper scales are in equilibrium.

How many blue weights should you add to the lowest scale to create equilibrium?

ANSWER: PAGE 125

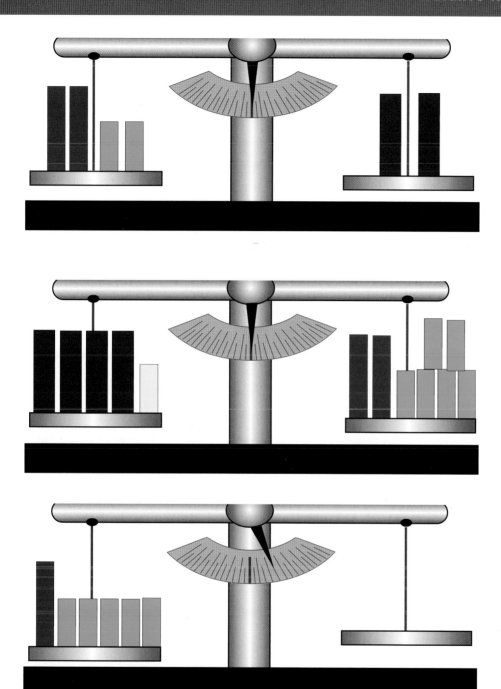

▲ WEIGHTY MATTERS 2

The two upper scales are in equilibrium.

How many blue and yellow weights should you add to the lowest scale to create equilibrium?

ANSWER: PAGE 125

This seems like a simple numbers game for two players, with either player having an equal opportunity to win. But is that the case? Play it and find out.

column 1	column 2
1	3
2	5
4	6
7	

▲ SUM-FREE GAME

Two players take turns placing consecutive numbers (starting with 1) in either of two columns.

The last player who can place a number in one of the columns without creating a sum of two numbers in that column is the winner.

In the sample game above, player two (red) loses, since he cannot place 8 in either column:

In column one, 1 + 7 = 8

In column two, 3 + 5 = 8

1) Can you work out a method by which player two can always win, no matter what player one does?

2) What is the longest possible game?

ANSWER: PAGE 125

▶ LUCAS'S SEQUENCE

Get a friend to write any two numbers in the two red squares (for example, 3 and 2), without showing them to you. Then let them write the sum of the two entries next to the number 2. and so on, telling you only the number that appears in the green square.

While they are doing that, you write the result (341) on a piece of paper and hand it to them.

How did you know the result in advance?

ANSWER: PAGE 125

1	
2	
3	
4	
5	
6	31
7	
8	
9	
sum:	

	3
1	2
2	5
3	7
4	12
5	19
6	31
7	50
8	81
9	131
sum:	341

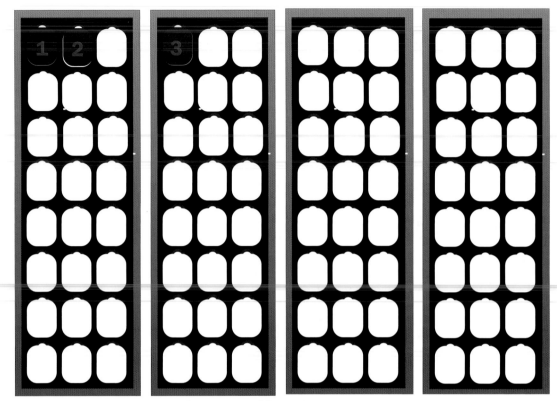

4 boxes

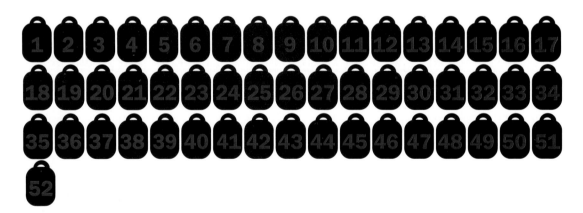

▲ WEIGHTS IN FOUR BOXES

How many consecutive weights (starting from 1) can you place in four boxes so that no box contains three weights of which one of the weights is the sum of other two?

We have placed the first three weights for you.

Can you place all 52?

ANSWER: PAGE 126

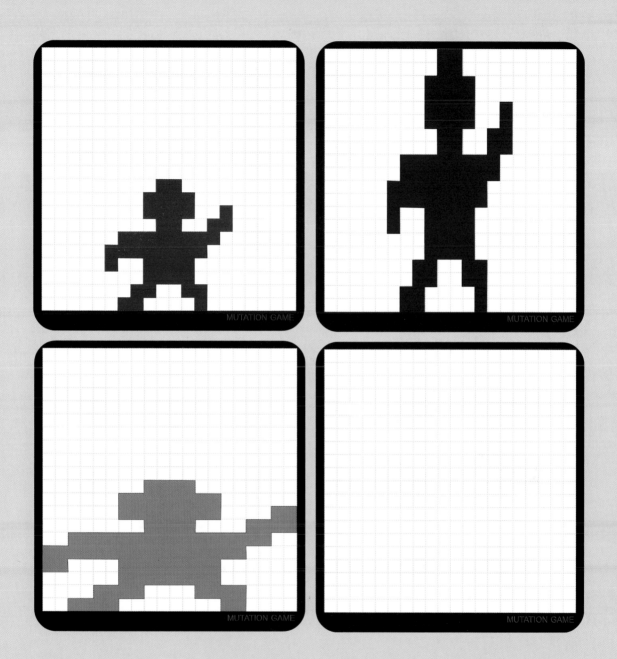

▲ MUTATIONS

Three out of a set of four cards based on a simple growth principle are shown. Can you draw the missing card?

ANSWER: PAGE 126

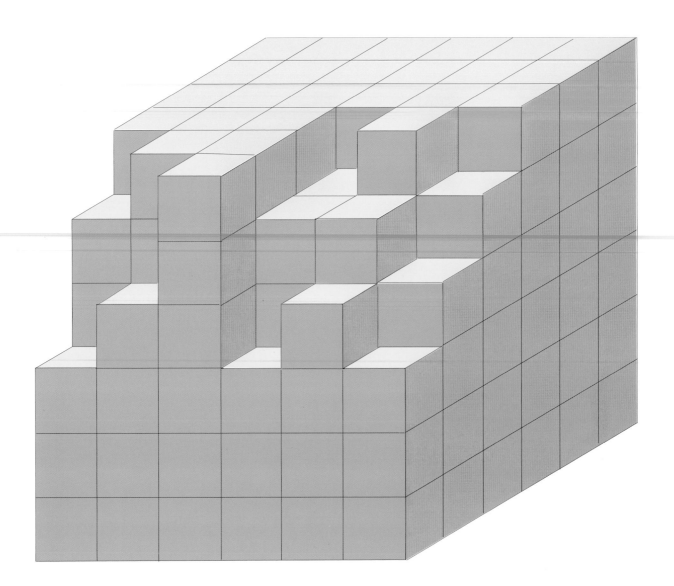

▲ MISSING CUBES

How many cubes are missing from the 6-by-6 cube stack?

ANSWER: PAGE 126

1

2

3

4

▲ CUBE STRUCTURES

Sixteen identical small cubes have been glued together to form each of the four structures.

Which has the largest surface area?

ANSWER: PAGE 126

▼ CUBE ORIENTATION

A cube can occupy its space in 24 different orientations, as shown below.
Fill in the missing colors.

ANSWER: PAGE 127

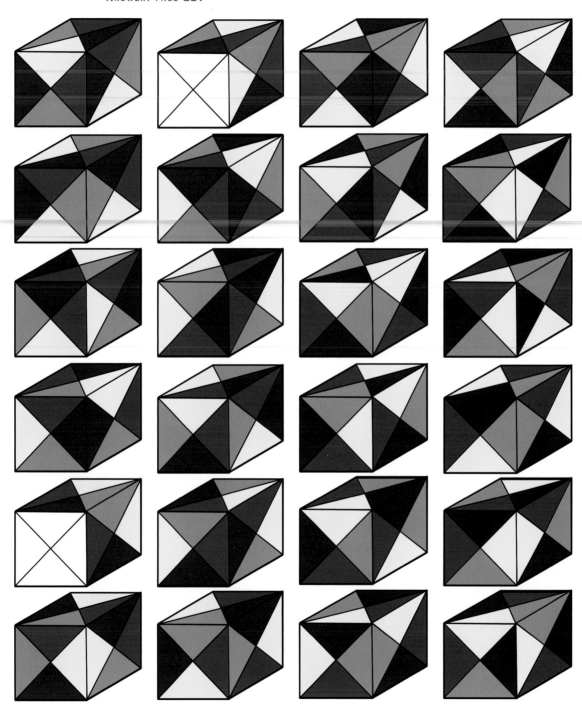

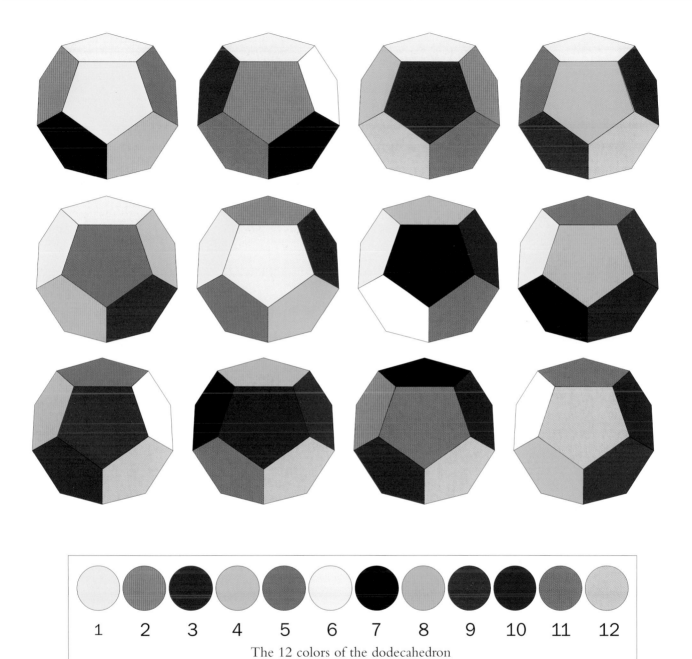

The 12 colors of the dodecahedron

▲ DODECAHEDRON ORIENTATION

Puzzle 1) In how many different ways can you place a dodecahedron on a table (occupying the same space each time)?

Puzzle 2) A single dodecahedron is shown in various orientations. Can you fill in the missing colors?

ANSWER: PAGE 127

▲ PAINTED CUBES

Eight cubes are joined into a 2 x 2 x 2 cube.

The 24 outer faces are to be painted with the least number of different colors necessary for any two squares with a common edge to have different colors.

How many colors will be needed?

ANSWER: PAGE 127

▲ PAINTED CUBES 2

A 3 x 3 x 3 cube is painted red on the outside and then cut into 27 unit cubes.

How many of the unit cubes will have 3 red faces, 2 red faces, 1 red face, or no painted sides at all?

ANSWER: PAGE 127

▼ CUBE DIAGONAL

The boy is playing with four identical giant cubes.

Using only his ruler, how can he find the length of one cube's diagonal?

ANSWER: PAGE 128

▼ MULTICUBE DIAGONAL

How can you find the length of the diagonal of a large cube made of eight separate cubes glued together? You are allowed to use separate, smaller cubes (each the size of one of the eight cubes used to make the large cube) to help you find the solution. How many smaller cubes will you need?

ANSWER: PAGE 128

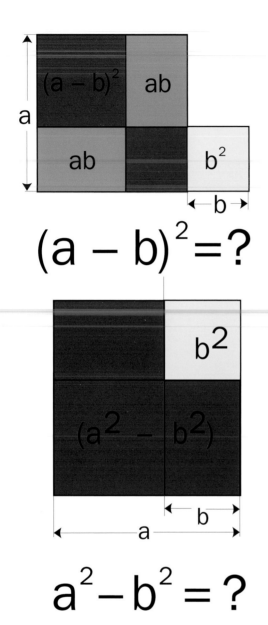

$$(a - b)^2 = ?$$

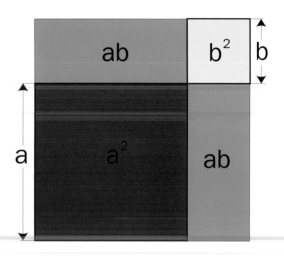

$$(a + b)^2 = ?$$

$$a^2 - b^2 = ?$$

▲ ALGEBRA

Too often we think of the rules of algebra as simply abstract and we forget that mathematics began for very practical and concrete reasons—for example, dividing land.

Can you work the simple algebraic problems shown above in their geometric illustrations?

ANSWER: PAGE 128

✳ Using letters for numbers

The term algebra derives from the Arabic "aljebr," adopted by the mathematician Al-Khowarizmi (died c. A.D. 850) to explain his ideas for solving equations. His two main operations in solving equations were:

1) The transposition of terms from one side of an equation to the other, and
2) The cancellation of equal terms appearing on opposite sides of an equation.

Algebra may seem entirely abstract, but it is possible to illustrate algebraic problems geometrically.

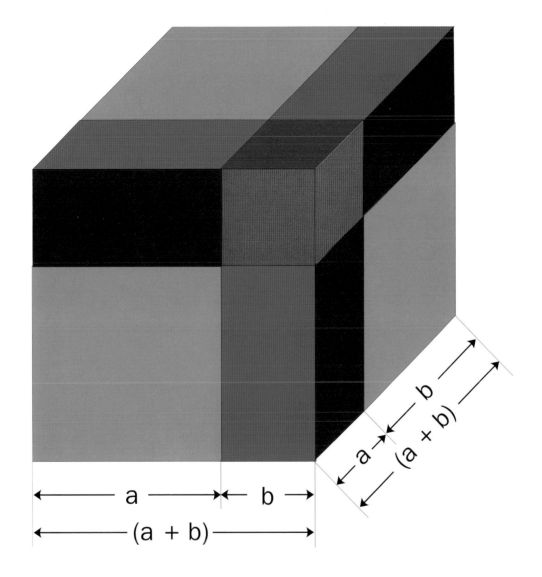

$$(a + b)^3 = ?$$

▲ BINOMIAL CUBE

One edge of the large cube is equal to (a + b), and the dissection pieces represent the expansion of (a + b)³.

The pieces corresponding to each kind of expansion term are colored differently. Can you work out the expansion in algebraic terms?

ANSWER: PAGE *128*

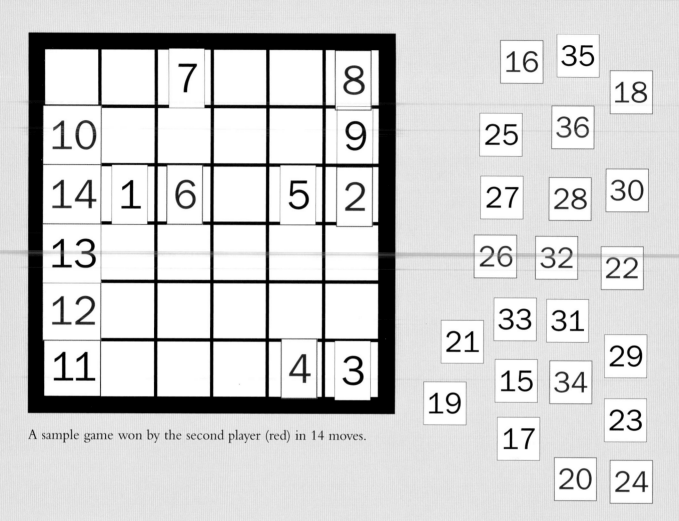

A sample game won by the second player (red) in 14 moves.

▲ PERSISTO

In this game, players take turns entering a number onto the game board, starting with 1 and continuing in consecutive numerical order. The first player (black) can place his or her 1 anywhere. Each subsequent number must be entered in either the same row or the same column (but not the same diagonal) as the previous one, but with the following restriction:

Only empty spaces may lie between the previous number and the one being entered. In other words, in proceeding to the next number you are not allowed to jump over a previous entry.

Whoever is the last person able to play a number wins the game.

LEVER PRINCIPLE (page 7)

The lever can change mechanical energy involving a small force into mechanical energy involving a large force. A heavy load is lifted a small distance by an effort five times less than would otherwise be required, which is the mechanical advantage of the machine. The effort is five times farther from the fulcrum than the load and will have to move five times as much as the load will move when the load is raised.

With a shovel, for instance, you push the handle a long way and make the blade move a short way—but with an increased force, so that you can lift a heavier load of soil. The spade turns, or pivots, low down on the ground.

HERO'S DOOR-OPENING MECHANISM (page 10)

Simple mechanical principles, using chains, pulleys, levers, and containers with air and water did the magic. The priest lit the fire on the altar. The air in the two containers is heated, expanding and pushing the water from the lower spherical container over a siphon into the hanging basket over a pulley. The descending basket will start pulling the ropes or chains, which will activate the hinges, making the doors "magically" open. When the fire is extinguished and everything cools down, the doors automatically close again, due to the action of the counterweight at the lower right.
(From the Latin edition of Hero's *Spiritalium Liber*, 1575.)

PERPETUAL MOTION MACHINES (page 8)

Leonardo's design is one of the most ancient gravitational perpetual motion machine concepts. The idea is that once the machine is started, the balls rolling in compartments will produce a greater momentum on the descending side of the wheel (where they are farther from the center) than the momentum of those on the ascending side (where they are nearer to the center). This will cause the wheel to rotate in a clockwise direction.

As successive weights were brought over the top, the theory went that they would fall down to the outer position and so keep the wheel turning. However, if we give the wheel a complete turn, so that each ball returns to its original position, the whole work done by the balls will, at the most, equal the input done on the wheel. The system can not gain energy during its motion. The wheel will not go on turning: it will only swing a bit and settle in a balanced position.

PERPETUAL MOBILE (page 10)

Gamow's idea was to attach sixes to the spokes of a wheel. Once set in motion the weight of the nines appearing on top would keep the wheel in motion eternally.

▶ MONKEY ON THE ROPE (page 11)

Any upward movements of the monkey and the bananas must be equal for the system to remain in equilibrium.

Diagram 1   Diagram 2

LIFT YOURSELF? (page 12)

The girl can, indeed, lift herself, if she is strong enough. If she weighs 60 pounds and the swing weighs 4 pounds, she can lift herself up by exerting 32 pounds of force on the rope.

PLATFORM UP (page 13)

It is theoretically possible, though it won't be easy. The boy must pull up with a force equal to his own weight plus the weight of the platform (and not lose his balance in the process).

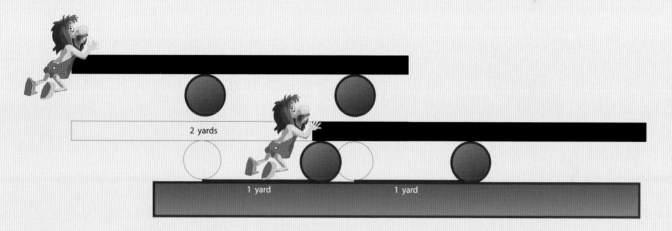

▲ ROLLER PRINCIPLE (page 14)

Surprisingly enough, the load always moves farther than the rollers.

If the roller rolls through one revolution, it advances forward a distance equal to pi times its diameter, while the load it supports moves forward a distance twice that distance, as shown above. This is because the load moves forward relative to the roller at the same time that the roller is moving forward on the ground.

If the rollers have a circumference of one yard, then the slab will move forward two yards per revolution.

This is called the "roller and slab" theroem.

GEAR CYCLE (page 15)

When the big gear revolves once, 14 teeth will be engaged on each gear. For all the gears to return to their initial positions, the big gear has to make n revolutions.

The gear with 13 teeth will make 14n/13 complete revolutions.

The gear with 12 teeth will make 14n/12 (7n/6) complete revolutions.

The gear with 11 teeth will make 14n/11 complete revolutions.

This means that n/13, n/6, and n/11 must be integers. The smallest positive value for n is therefore 13 x 6 x 11 = 858.

GEAR ANAGRAM (page 16)

"The impossible takes longer."

The sentence will appear at the contact points of the gears when the large top red gear makes $\frac{1}{8}$ of a revolution clockwise.

(According to *Respectfully Quoted: A Dictionary of Quotations*, this quote by an unknown author is part of an inscription on the Seabees Memorial, which reads, "The difficult we do at once; the impossible takes a bit longer.")

▶ GEAR SWITCHING (page 17)

The small yellow gear will activate the vertical rack, pushing it downward 18 teeth to activate the switch after 6 minutes.

The green gear will activate the horizontal rack, pushing it 12 teeth to the left to activate the switch after 3 minutes.

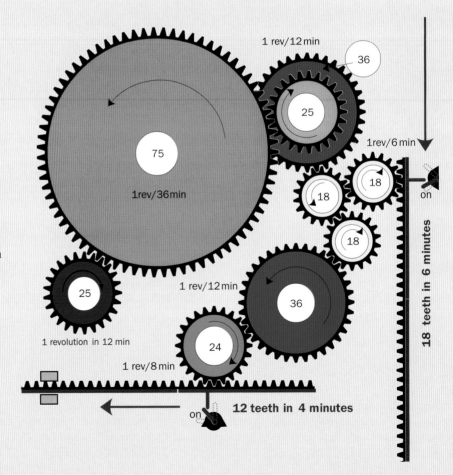

▲ GEAR PUZZLE (page 18)

If you turn the middle gear just one color counterclockwise, all the touching colors will match.

▲ GEAR HEXAGON (page 20)

Two-thirds of a revolution counterclockwise.

▲ GEAR SQUARE (page 19)

Two and a half revolutions counterclockwise.

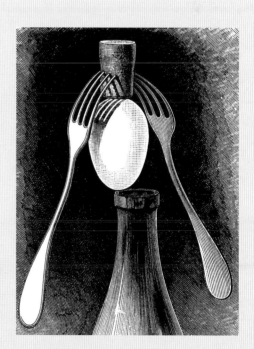

▲ THE COLUMBUS EGG (page 21)

(from *Kolumbus-Egg,* published 1890) The egg is balanced on the same principle that tightrope walkers use to walk on a stretched rope. The two forks provide counterweights far below the egg, lowering the center of gravity. With a bit of patience the feat as shown in the illustration above can be achieved.

OFFSET BLOCKS (page 22)

In theory, the structure could be built as high as you want. As you place the blocks on one another, the upper block will not fall as long as its center of gravity is above the next lower block.

If all the blocks are placed perfectly, the structure will stay stable and balanced on the bottom blocks. (Of course, in reality, small errors would creep into the structure at some point, causing it to topple.)

▶ CHANCE BALANCE (page 23)

There are six different equilibrium situations (the three shown at right and their reflections).

The probability of random equilibrium is 6/120 = 1/20.

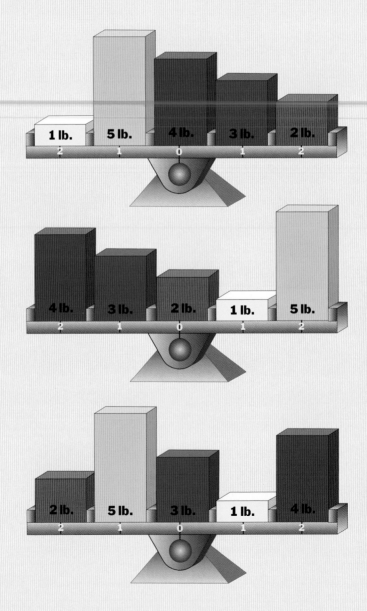

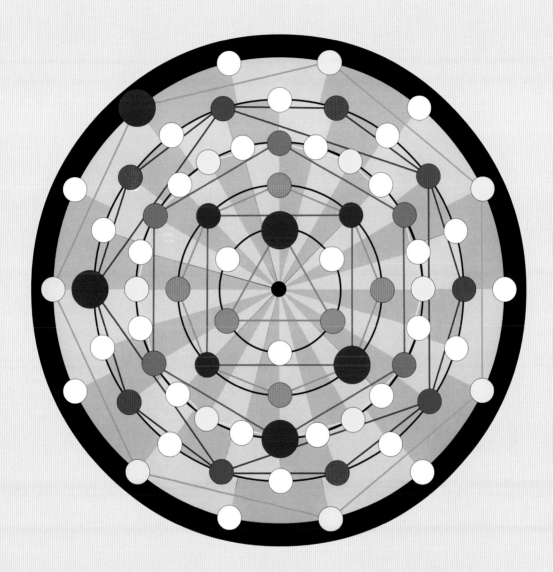

▲ BALANCING PLATFORM (page 24)

The weights placed on the platform are at the vertices of regular
polygons, with weights missing at five vertices. Adding the missing
weights (big red circles) will create equilibrium about the center pivot
because the weights will be symmetrically distributed.

▶ **MENTAL IMBALANCE**
(page 25)

There are alternate solutions.

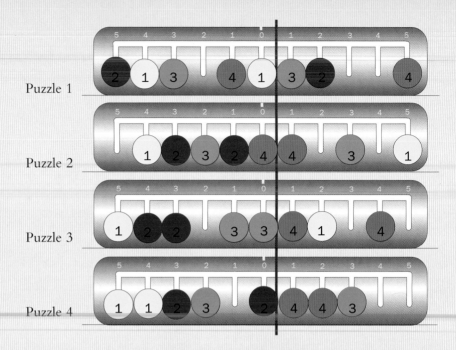

To calculate the turning force (moment) on each side, we use the formula: weight × distance from pivot. In puzzle 1, on the right-hand side we have:
Blue weight: 5 × 4 = 20 units
Red weight: 2 × 2 = 4 units
Green weight: 3 × 1 = 3 units

That's a total force of 27 units. On the left-hand side, we have (2 × 5) + (1 × 4) + (3 × 3) + (4 × 1) + (1 × 0) = 10 + 4 + 9 + 4 + 0 = 27 units. This is the same as the right side, so that the system balances.

▼ **REGULAR TESSELLATIONS (page 26)**

One of the most astonishingly counterintuitive facts of geometry is that there are only three possible regular tessellations. They have as their elements equilateral triangles, squares, and regular hexagons.

There is a beautiful geometrical logic behind the rarity of regular tessellations. Since their basic elements are regular polygons, one condition must be fulfilled: at every meeting point of such polygons (vertices), the sum of all their angles must be 360 degrees. An equilateral triangle has angles at 60 degrees;

therefore exactly six such triangles can meet in a vertex. A square has angles at 90 degrees; therefore exactly four squares can meet in a vertex.

A regular hexagon has angles of 120 degrees; therefore exactly three such hexagons can meet in a vertex.

No other regular polygon, no matter how many sides it has, can tessellate the plane in a regular fashion—there are only three regular tessellations.

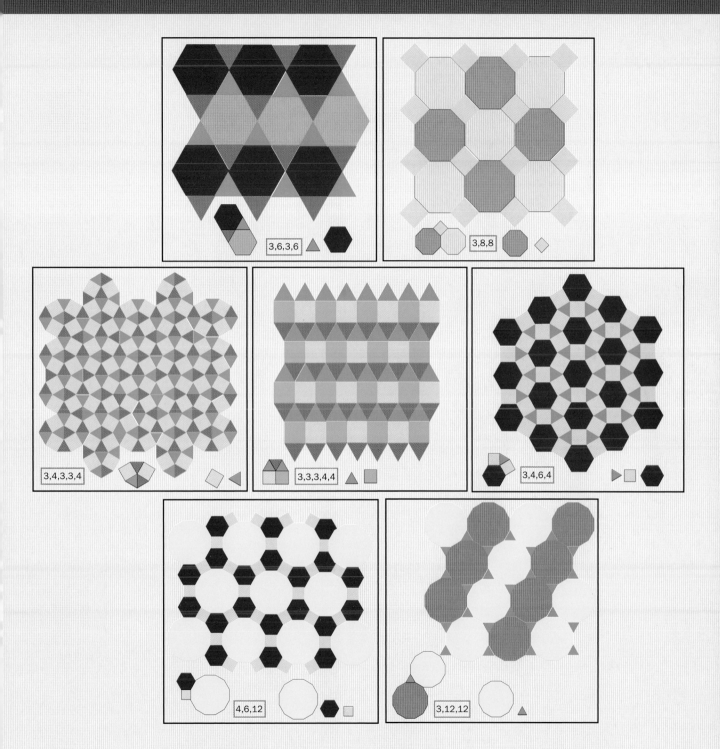

▲ **SEMIREGULAR TESSELLATIONS (page 27)**

The other seven semiregular tessellations.

**◄ PINWHEEL TRIANGLES AND SUPER-TILING
(page 28)**
A 625-unit pinwheel triangle. Can you fill in the
outlines of the five 125-unit pinwheel triangles?

▼ **TESSELLATING PENTAGONS (page 29)**

Other solutions exist.

▼ **OVERLAPPING TESSELLATION (page 31)**

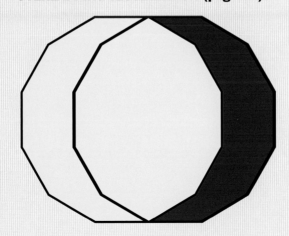

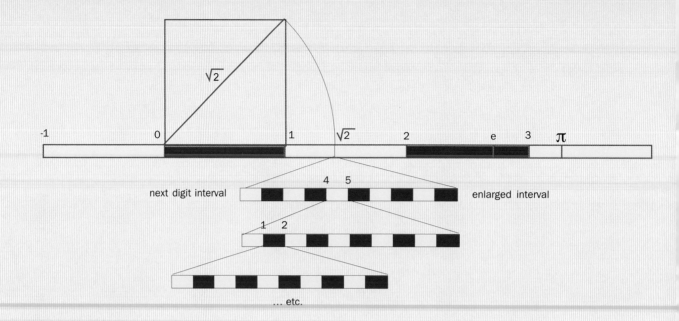

▲ NUMBER LINE (page 33)

The number line is a very densely populated line. There are no gaps or holes in it. It flows smoothly and continuously containing an infinite number of real numbers. All the rational and irrational numbers can be found on the number line.

GALLERY OF NUMBERS (page 34)

An odd number times an odd number results in an odd number, and so any power of an odd number is odd. All the first terms are odd. All the paintings except the second are in evenistic style.

NUMBER SELECTION (page 35)

No matter how you choose the 10 numbers, there will always be two completely different sets that will add up to the same sum.

There are 10 ways of choosing one number, $(10 \times 9) \div (2 \times 1)$ ways of choosing a group of two numbers, $(10 \times 9 \times 8) \div (3 \times 2 \times 1)$ ways of choosing three numbers, and so on up to $(10 \times 9 \times 8 \times 7 \times 6 \times 5 \times 4 \times 3 \times 2) \div (9 \times 8 \times 7 \times 6 \times 5 \times 4 \times 3 \times 2 \times 1)$ (i.e. 10) ways of choosing 9 numbers. That's a total of 1,012 possible sets.

The minimum possible sum for a subset is 1. The maximum possible sum for ten digits is 945 (90 to 99 totaled).

This means that there are only 944 different possible results but 1,012 ways of choosing our numbers.

Therefore, for any set of 10 whole numbers chosen from under 100, there will always be at least one way of finding two subsets with the same total.

SUMS TO TEN (page 36)

The number of different ways to divide up a rod of length n is $2^{(n-1)}$.

$2 \times 2 \times 2 \times 2 \times 2 \times 2 \times 2 \times 2 \times 2 = 512$

Imagine that the 10-unit rod is marked at 1-unit intervals. At each interval, one of two things can happen—you can break the rod, or leave it intact.

There are nine points at which you could break the rod or leave it intact, so there are 2^9 ways of arranging the rods to form 10-unit lengths.

▼ CUISENAIRE PUZZLE (page 36)

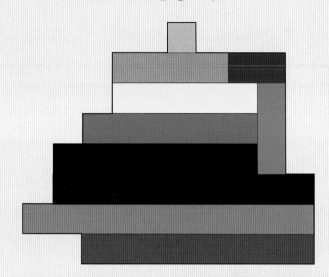

DIGITS 1 TO 9 (page 37)

$32,547,891 \times 6 = 195,287,346$

▼ ROTATING OBJECT (page 38)

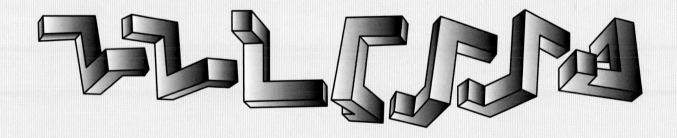

ORBITAL ILLUSION (page 39)

Kepler was certainly right, but our ellipse is not really an ellipse. On its middle part there are two parallel straight lines which seem to be distorted by the overlapping radial lines. Thus it appears that we are looking at an elliptical orbit.

▼ PLAYING THE TRIANGLE (page 41)

Gauss recognized that there are 50 sums of 101 in the sequence of numbers from 1 to 100 (1 + 100, 2 + 99, 3 + 98, and so on to 50 + 51), which gives a total of 5050. An example of this on a smaller scale (using the numbers 1 to 10) is shown below.

Gauss's feat works for any number n, not just for 100, according to the general pattern:

$$1 + 2 + 3 + \ldots + n = n(n + 1)/2$$

This general formula is also the formula for triangular numbers.

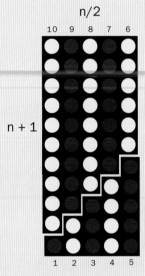

THREE-DIMENSIONAL FIGURATE NUMBERS (page 42)

Tetrahedral numbers: 1, 4, 10, 20, 35, 56, 84. Each element of this series is expressed by the formula $1/6\, n\, (n + 1)\, (n + 2)$.

Pyramidal numbers: 1, 5, 14, 30, 55, 91, 140. Each element of this series is expressed by the formula $1/6\, n\, (n + 1)\, (2n + 1)$.

n is the number of spheres along an edge. Each layer of the big pyramid contains n^2 spheres.

The number of spheres in the bottom layer is 100. The total number of spheres in the pyramid is

$$1 + 4 + 9 + 16 + 25 + 36 + 49 + 64 + 81 + 100 = 385.$$

PIGGY BANK (page 43)

$$\tfrac{1}{4}x + \tfrac{1}{5}x + \tfrac{1}{6}x = 37$$

$$\frac{(15 + 12 + 10)}{60}\, x = 37$$

x = 60, so I saved $60.

▼ WORD SQUARES (page 45)

Many other solutions are possible.

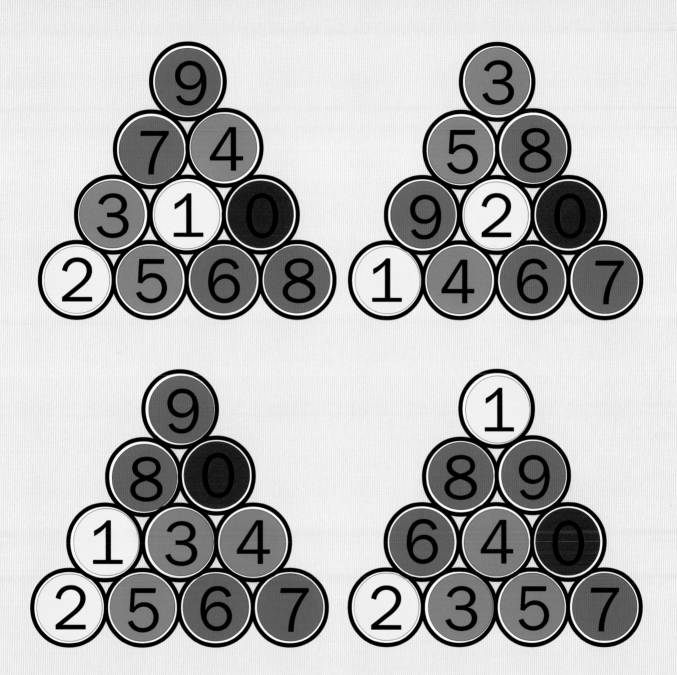

▲ TRIANGULAR NUMBERS (page 46)

Charles W. Trigg found that there are 136 essentially different triangular arrangements which have like digit-sums along the three sides. Four possible solutions are shown.

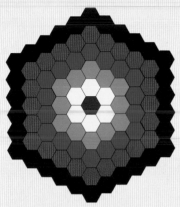

Sixth centered hexagonal
number ($H_6 = 91$)

First centered hexagonal
number ($H_1 = 1$)

Second centered hexagonal
number ($H_2 = 7$)

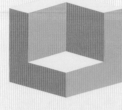

Third centered hexagonal
number ($H_3 = 19$)

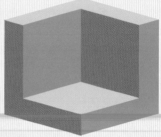

Fourth centered hexagonal
number ($H_4 = 37$)

▶ CENTERED HEXAGONAL NUMBERS (page 47)

1) The sixth hexagonal number is 91.
The general formula:

$$H_n = n^3 - (n - 1)^3$$

2) The sum of the first six hexagonal numbers is 216, which is a cube of side six, as shown. Interestingly enough, the sums of consecutive hexagonal numbers are always cubes.
The general formula:

$$H_1 + H_2 + \ldots + H_n = n^3$$

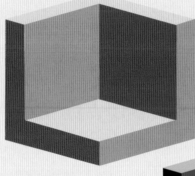

Fifth centered hexagonal
number ($H_5 = 61$)

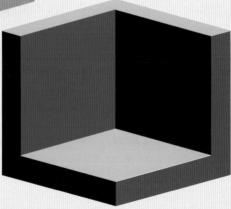

Sixth centered hexagonal
number ($H_6 = 91$)

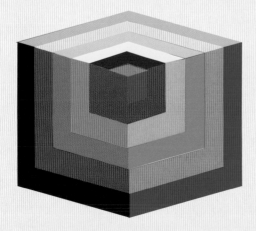

The sum of the first six centered hexagonal numbers—
a perfect 6-by-6-by-6 cube

IRRATIONAL (page 48)

The proof is actually quite simple: Assume $\sqrt{2} = P/Q$, and that the fraction has been reduced (meaning that P and Q have no common factors). Squaring this equation, we get:

$P^2 = 2Q^2$, which tells us that P is an even number, of a form $P = 2R$. Substituting this into $P^2 = 2Q^2$ we get $2R^2 = Q^2$ which tells us that Q is also an even number, contrary to our initial assumption that P and Q have no common factors. This contradiction indicates that such natural numbers P and Q don't exist.

The number $\sqrt{2}$ is an irrational number, which means it cannot be expressed as a ratio of two whole numbers. It is the number which, when multiplied by itself, gives the answer 2. If we try to write it in decimal form the sequence of digits does not end, and there is no pattern of repetition, as there would be in a repeating decimal whose digits also go on infinitely, but can be predicted, for example:

⅓ = 0.33333333, or 24282/99999 = 0.2428124281

Computers have been used to calculate $\sqrt{2}$ to thousands of digits, but so far no evidence of any pattern or repetition has been found.

▼ ADDITION (page 49)

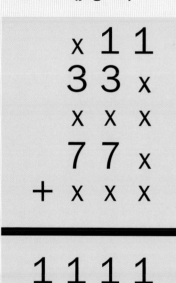

▼ EIGHT EIGHTS (page 49)

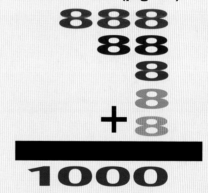

▼ ADD UP TO 15 (page 49)

Eight groups.

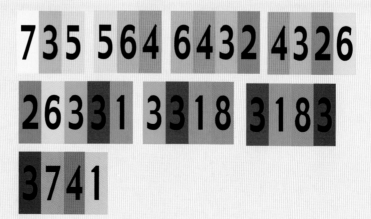

▶ **HIROIMONO (page 50)**

One of the many possible solutions.

DIVISIBILITY (page 51)

The answer is 2,520 = 5 × 7 × 8 × 9. If a number is divisible by 8, it will be divisible by 2 and 4 automatically. The same follows for 3 if it is divisible by 9. If it is divisible by 2 and 3, it will be divisible by 6 also.

DIVISIBILITY AGAIN (page 51)

348,926,128 is divisible by 4 and 8
845,386,720 is divisible by 4 and 8
457,873,804 is divisible by 4
567,467,334 is not divisible by 4 or 8
895,623,724 is divisible by 4

If the last two digits of a number are evenly divisible by four, the number can be divided by four. If the last three digits of a number are evenly divisible by eight, the number is divisible by eight.

The Hiroimono solution grid shows the following numbers arranged in connected cells:

Top: 3, 4, 5
Next row: 1, 2, 8, 6, 7
Below: 9
Then: 11, 10, 12
Then: 15, 14, 13
Then: 19, 18, 17, 16, 25, 26, 27, 28, 29
Then: 20, 21, 22, 23, 24, 33, 32, 31, 30
Then: 38, 39, 34
Then: 37, 36, 35
Then: 40

▼ **LAGRANGE'S THEOREM (page 51)**

$$35 = 25 + 9 + 1$$

$$48 = 36 + 4 + 4 + 4$$

▼ **NUMBER LABYRINTHS (page 52)**

5	6	23	24	25
4	7	22	21	20
3	8	17	18	19
2	9	16	15	14
1	10	11	12	13

15	14	13	12	3	2
16	23	24	11	4	1
17	22	25	10	5	6
18	21	26	9	8	7
19	20	27	28	29	30
36	35	34	33	32	31

◀ **BIG LABYRINTH (page 53)**

99	100	95	94	81	80	73	72	69	68
98	97	96	93	82	79	74	71	70	67
89	90	91	92	83	78	75	64	65	66
88	87	86	85	84	77	76	63	62	61
13	14	29	30	31	32	33	34	35	60
12	15	28	27	26	25	24	23	36	59
11	16	17	18	19	20	21	22	37	58
10	45	44	43	42	41	40	39	38	57
9	46	47	48	49	50	51	52	53	56
8	7	6	5	4	3	2	1	54	55

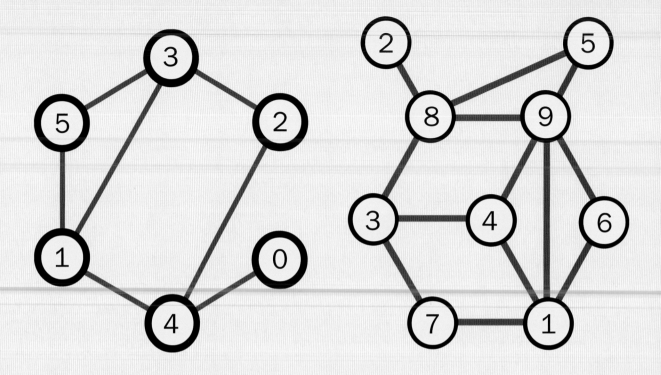

▲ **NUMBER NEIGHBORS (page 54)**   ▲ **NUMBER NEIGHBORS 2 (page 55)**

**NUMBER SUMS AND DIFFERENCES
(page 56)**
There are two essentially different solutions:
    4 1 5 4 1 3 2 5 3 2
    4 5 1 4 3 1 2 3 5 2
Two other solutions can be obtained by
reversing the orders of the sequences.

NUMBER SEQUENCE (page 57)
Square numbers are omitted.

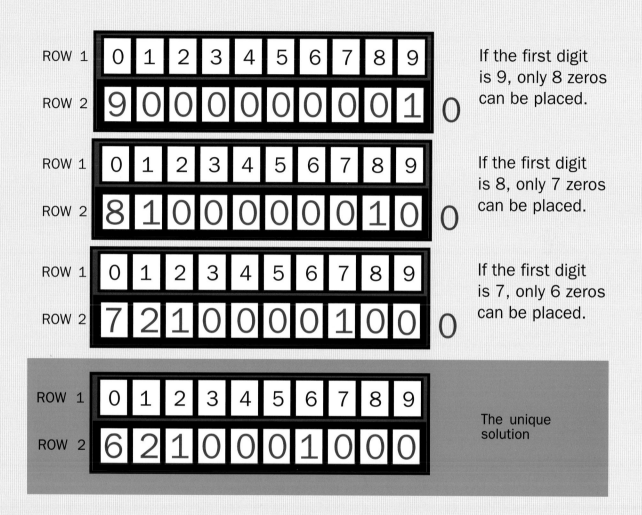

ROW 1 | 0 1 2 3 4 5 6 7 8 9
ROW 2 | 9 0 0 0 0 0 0 0 1 0

If the first digit is 9, only 8 zeros can be placed.

ROW 1 | 0 1 2 3 4 5 6 7 8 9
ROW 2 | 8 1 0 0 0 0 0 0 1 0 0

If the first digit is 8, only 7 zeros can be placed.

ROW 1 | 0 1 2 3 4 5 6 7 8 9
ROW 2 | 7 2 1 0 0 0 0 1 0 0 0

If the first digit is 7, only 6 zeros can be placed.

ROW 1 | 0 1 2 3 4 5 6 7 8 9
ROW 2 | 6 2 1 0 0 0 1 0 0 0

The unique solution

▲ **SELF-DESCRIPTIVE NUMBER (page 58)**

If we start systematically, entering 9 as the first digit and filling in the other numbers as needed, we can see it won't work, since 9 zeros cannot be placed; 8 and 7 have similar results, as shown above. Entering 6 as the first digit quickly gives the correct solution.

KAPREKAR'S MAGIC (page 59)

You will always end up with 6,174.

D. R. Kaprekar discovered the existence of numbers such as this and they are called Kaprekar's constants in his honor.

If you start with a two-digit number you will end up cycling through these 5 numbers: 9, 81, 63, 27, 45.

If you start with a three-digit number you will end up with 495.

▶ CARDS AROUND (page 60)

Consider any four cards. The first three cards of the four must total 21, as must the final three cards. This means the first and last cards must be the same. If they were not, both triplets of cards couldn't add up to the same total. This explains why every third card must is the same value.

CALCULATOR TROUBLE (page 61)

Three one-digit numbers: 1, 2, 3.

3^2 or 9 two-digit numbers: 11, 12, 13, 21, 22, 23, 31, 32, 33.

3^3 or 27 three-digit numbers: 111, 112, 113, 121, 122, 123, 131, 132, 133, 211, 212, 213, 221, 222, 223, 231, 232, 233, 311, 312, 313, 321, 322, 323, 331, 332, 333.

Altogether, 39 numbers can be made, which can be derived from the general formula:

$$3 + 3^2 + 3^3 = 39$$

$2 = {}^{44}\!/_{44}$

$2 = {}^4\!/_4 + {}^4\!/_4$

$3 = (4 + 4 + 4)/4$

$4 = 4 (4 - 4) + 4$

$5 = ((4 \times 4) + 4) / 4$

$6 = 4 + ((4 + 4) / 4)$

$7 = 4 + 4 - ({}^4\!/_4)$

$8 = 4 + 4 + 4 - 4$

$9 = 4 + 4 + ({}^4\!/_4)$

$10 = (44 - 4) \sqrt{4}$

$11 = 44 / \sqrt{4} \times \sqrt{4}$

$12 = (44 + 4)/4$

$13 = ({}^{44}\!/_4) + \sqrt{4}$

$14 = 4 + 4 + 4 \sqrt{4}$

$15 = ({}^{44}\!/_4) + 4$

$16 = 4 + 4 + 4 + 4$

$17 = (4 \times 4) + {}^4\!/_4$

$18 = (4 \times 4) + 4 - \sqrt{4}$

$19 = $ Impossible

$20 = (4 \times 4) + \sqrt{4} + \sqrt{4}$

▶ PALINDROMES (page 61)

Sorry if I caused you to do a lot of work to finally produce a palindrome!

Martin Gardner noted that of the first 10,000 numbers, only 251 of them do not produce a palindromic number in less than 23 steps. It was once conjectured that all numbers would eventually produce a palindrome. This conjecture has been proven false.

Among the first 100,000 numbers, 5,996 numbers never generate a palindrome, the first being 196.

◀ FOUR FOURS (page 62)

The only number less than 20 that cannot be expressed within the restrictions is 19. If we allow factorials to be used ($4! = 1 \times 2 \times 3 \times 4 = 24$), 19 can be expressed as $19 = 4! - 4 - ({}^4\!/_4)$

89
98
187
781
968
869
1837
7381
9218
8129
17347
74371
91718
81719
173437
734371
907808
808709
1716517
7156171
8872688
8862788
17735476
67453771
85189247
74298158
159487405
504784951
664272356
653272466
1317544822
2284457131
3602001953
3591002063
7193004016
6104003917
13297007933
33970079231
47267087164
46178076274
93445163438
83436154439
176881317877
778713188671
955594506548
845605495559
1801200002107
7012000021081

Finally—a palindrome! 8813200023188

FOUR-DIGIT MUTANTS (page 63)

$4 + 4^2 + 4^3 + 4^4 = 340$

▼ NUMBER SEQUENCE (page 64)

The sequence consists of ascending numbers that don't change value when they are turned upside-down.

▼ SOCCER BALL (page 65)

5 ounces is one quarter of the weight of the soccer ball, which weighs 20 ounces.

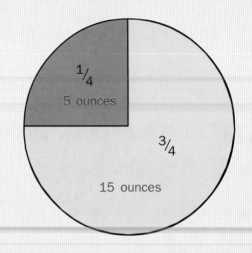

▼ MATH EXPRESSIONS (page 66)

The seven math expressions in descending order.

$$10^2 = 100$$

$$10$$

$$\frac{10}{\sqrt{10}} = 3.1622777 \qquad \sqrt{10} = 3.1622777$$

$$\frac{\sqrt{10}}{10} = 0.3162277 \qquad \frac{1}{\sqrt{10}} = 0.3162277$$

$$\frac{1}{10\sqrt{10}} = 0.0316227$$

▼ HALF OF ELEVEN (page 67)

VI is 6 in Roman numerals.

▼ ADD A LINE (page 67)

545+5=550

▼ THINK OF A NUMBER (page 68)

Ancient Egyptian mathematicians knew about fixed unknown numbers, calling them "heeps."

We shall borrow this idea, and instead of specifying the value of our number we shall consider it as a "heep" (black box). By following along with the instructions, the secret of the trick will reveal itself in all its simplicity. You will accomplish two things:

1) You will work with a number without knowing its value. That is algebra (in which our "heep" would be denoted by a variable such as "x").

2) Instead of checking specific numbers to see if they work, you will find the problem in general mathematical interpretation, which shows that the trick must always work.

There are many instances in algebra and mathematics in general in which complicated proofs can be visualized with geometric diagrams, conveying the proof of a theorem at a glance.

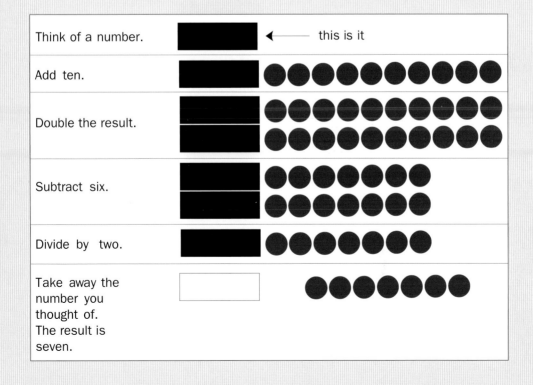

THE LIKENESS SEQUENCE (page 69)

Ninth generation: 31131211131221

Tenth generation: 13211311123113112211.

Each term in the sequence describes the previous one (three 1s, one 3, one 2, one 1, and so on).

The sequence grows very rapidly, and never contains a number greater than 3.

For example, the 16th generation has 102 numbers, while the 27th generation contains 2,012 numbers.

The sequence was described by Mario Hilgemeier, a German mathematician, in 1980.

HAILSTONE NUMBERS (page 70)

Seven will lead to the loop, although it takes a little longer: 7, 22, 11, 34, 17, 52, 26, 13, 40, 20, 10, 5, 16, 8, 4, 2, 1, 4, 2, ...

It is not yet known if every number will fall into the same loop.

None of the numbers from 1 to 26 survive very long, but 27 takes us on quite a long ride. It goes up to 9,232 at the 77th step, its highest point, and finally reaches the loop at the 111th step.

Physicist Malcolm E. Lines, in his exciting book *Think of a Number*, mentions that all numbers up to one trillion have been tested by the University of Tokyo, and every one of them collapses to the 142142 loop.

PERSISTENCE OF NUMBERS (page 71)

The smallest numbers with persistence numbers of 2, 3, and 4, are 25, 39, and 77 respectively. Every starting number leads to a single digit; the process is not infinite.

Persistence	Lowest number
1	10
2	25
3	39
4	77
5	679
6	6788
7	68889
8	2677889
9	26888999
10	3778888999
11	277777788888899

Note the abundance of 8s and 9s.

Why so many? No one knows.

▼ **DIFFERENCE HEXAGONS (page 72)**

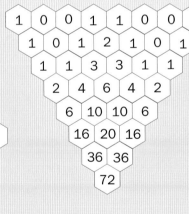

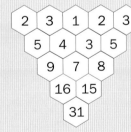

▶ **LADYBUG GARDEN (page 74)**
One of the possible solutions.

▼ **NUMBER CARDS (page 75)**

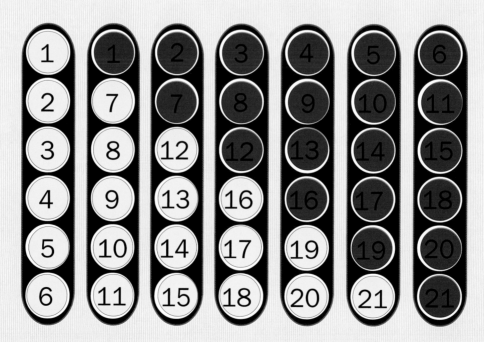

▶ RUNNING ORDER (page 76)

| 8th | 7th | 6th | 5th | 4th | 3rd | 2nd | 1st |

This is the unique solution for four pairs. Problems like this are called Langford's problems.

   In general, if n is the number of pairs, the problem has a solution only if n is a multiple of 4 or one less than such a multiple.

RUNNING TRIPLETS (page 77)

3 4 7 9 3 6 4 8 3 5 7 4 6 9 2 5 8 2 7 6 2 5 1 9 1 8 1

CONSECUTIVE WEIGHTS (page 78)

Puzzle 1) The weights are 17, 18, and 19 grams.
Puzzle 2) x + (x + 1) + (x + 2) + (x + 3) = 90
$$4x + 6 = 90$$
$$x = 21$$
The numbers are 21, 22, 23, and 24.

EQUATION BALANCE (page 79)

$$4 - x = x - 2$$
$$6 = 2x$$
$$3 = x$$

WEIGHTY MATTERS 1 & 2 (pages 80–81)

1) Seven blue weights.
2) Three blue weights and one yellow weight.

▼ SUM-FREE GAME (page 82)

Problem 1) No matter which column player one places the number 5 in, player two wins by placing the 6 in the other column.

column 1	column 2
1	3
2	4
5	6

column 1	column 2
1	3
2	4
6	5

column 1	column 2
1	3
2	5
4	6
8	7

Problem 2) It is impossible to place nine numbers in this game. The longest game is eight moves long.

LUCAS'S SEQUENCE (PAGE 83)

The sum of the 10 numbers is always 11 times the number in the green square, whatever numbers are chosen for the first two numbers.

▼ WEIGHTS IN FOUR BOXES (page 84)

All 52 weights can be placed. Other solutions are possible.

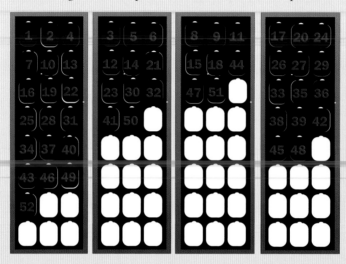

▼ MUTATIONS (page 85)

The missing card is shown below. The original shape has been doubled in both height and width.

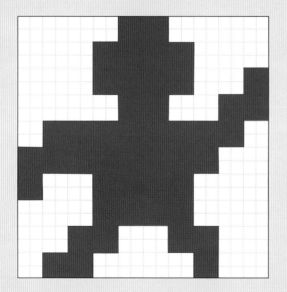

MISSING CUBES (page 86)

Twenty cubes are missing.

CUBE STRUCTURES (page 87)

To find the surface areas, count the number of faces that are glued together and subtract from 96 (the total number of faces of the 16 cubes).

Structure 2 has the largest surface area because only 15 pairs of faces are glued together.

▶ CUBE ORIENTATION (page 88)

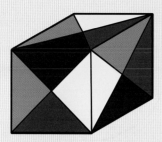

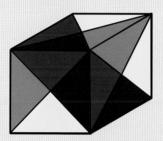

▶ PAINTED CUBES (page 90)

The eight cubes can be easily colored on a 2-dimensional "Schlegel diagram," which is topologically equivalent to the three-dimensional cubes.

Three different colors are necessary as shown.

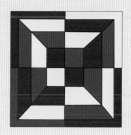

PAINTED CUBES 2 (page 91)

Cubes painted red on three faces: 8
Cubes painted red on two faces: 12
Cubes painted red on one face: 6
Unpainted cubes: 1

▶ DODECAHEDRON ORIENTATION (page 89)

Puzzle 1) There are 12 faces which can each be oriented 5 different ways, so there are 60 different possible orientations.

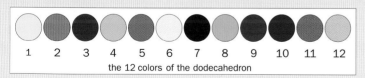

1 2 3 4 5 6 7 8 9 10 11 12
the 12 colors of the dodecahedron

Puzzle 2) The missing colors are shown below.

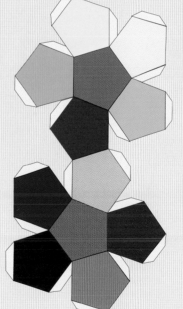

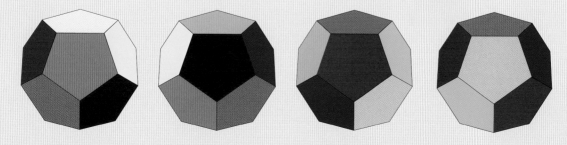

▼ CUBE DIAGONAL (page 92)

He arranged three cubes as below and measured the line x as shown.

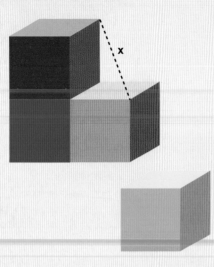

▲ BINOMIAL CUBE (page 95)

$$(a + b)^3 = a^3 + 3a^2 b + 3ab^2 + b^3$$

▼ MULTICUBE DIAGONAL (page 92)

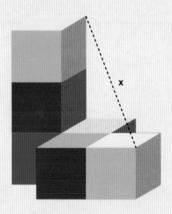

Six cubes are sufficient to recreate the physical space of the original cube and so measure the length of the diagonal.

▼ ALGEBRA (page 94)

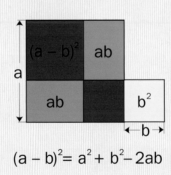

$$(a - b)^2 = a^2 + b^2 - 2ab$$

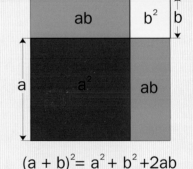

$$(a + b)^2 = a^2 + b^2 + 2ab$$

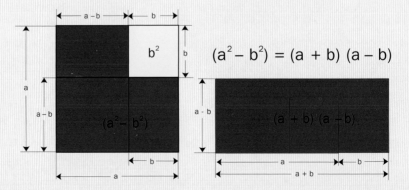

$$(a^2 - b^2) = (a + b)(a - b)$$